What others are sayi

Their words inspire, cajo ....uy enthuse. *Cruising 101* has helped me keep the dream alive. Read it and renew your dreams. — *Roy Huntington, the Informant*

We receive scores of books from just-returned cruisers. In most cases, the strongest aspect of the books is the sincerity of the author(s)...*Cruising 101* is the rare exception. The couple are not only observant and insightful, they know how to write...a fine new book. — *Richard Spindler, Latitude 38°*

Cruising 101 answers a lot of questions and paints many pictures for those yet to experience their first cruise, and articulates for many seasoned veterans what can go wrong if they are not prepared. But what it gives most is the motivation to cruise out and stake your own claim to a small piece of paradise.—*Sea, America's Western Boating Magazine*

Cruising 101 is exactly what the words imply...but the volume is more...the authors dare to talk about those aspects of long distance sailing which are usually left unsaid...a little gem of a book. — *The Log*

Cruising is a life altering experience whether you do it for a year or the rest of your life. That is the lesson of *Cruising 101*... An insightful, upbeat and practical book. They offer sound advice, encouragement, and caution... but always with the admonition to act on your dreams. —*Dockside*

They have a refreshingly creative style and no nonsense approach to these lessons for 'freshmen cruisers' that make *Cruising 101* one of the best books I have read. — *Susan Straubing, Sister Sail, A Forum for Women Afloat*

They have managed to combine an intriguing memoir with an informative how-to book. *Cruising 101* should be on the reading list of any first time cruiser. —*Jennifer & Russell Redmond, Sea of Cortez Review*

Cruising 101 navigates issues that were previously uncharted waters... A must read for first time cruisers. — *Chris Frost, Downwind Marine*

In Loving Memory of
Jeff and Scott Lepak

Cruising 101

Avoiding the Pitfalls of Paradise

By Amy Sullivan and Kevin Donnelly

Free Fall Press
San Diego • 1997

Cruising 101
Avoiding the Pitfalls of Paradise

By Amy Sullivan and Kevin Donnelly

Published by:

Free Fall Press
Post Office Box 7887
San Diego, CA 92167
www.freefallpress.com

Photography by Amy Sullivan
Cover Design by Court Patton

ISBN: 0-9658247-8-0
Library of Congress Catalog Card Number: 97-60947

Acknowledgment

Writing a book took the same amount of commitment as cruising, and we encountered just as many miracles.

We would like to give special thanks to those who helped us cross our mountains in this effort. To Court Patton, whose guidance gave us direction, along with a face for our cover. Special thanks to Robert E. Gibson, our editor, impartial observer and spare pair of eyes.

And for all the support, love and constant laughs from our extended cruising family and the Hidden Port Yacht Club, we are forever thankful.

Table of Contents

Chapter 6

Boat Modifications: Hindsight is better than no sight.

Chapter 7

Things to Bring: And a guide for things best left at home.

Chapter 8

Provisioning: Food for the body, mind, and other living things.

Chapter 9

The Cruising Budget: How much is this in dollars, por favor?

Chapter 10

About the People: It takes all kinds to stock a planet.

Chapter 11

The Cruising Etiquette: Surefire ways to get invited to the dance.

Chapter 12

On the Road to Paradise: The world you take is the world you'll make.

Disclaimer

The decision to go cruising is an individual one, and must be made with the full awareness that it does entail an element of risk, including loss of property, injury, or loss of life. Therefore, this text should be used as a general guide and not as an ultimate source of cruising or sailing information.

The purpose of this book is to educate and entertain. The authors and Free Fall Press hold no liability or responsibility to any person or entity with respect to any loss or damage caused, or alleged to be caused, directly or indirectly by the information contained in this book.

If you do not wish to be bound by the above, you may return this book to the publisher for a full refund.

Preface

The Winds of Change

They left it all, like some of us,
in answer to the call...
—Kevin Donnelly

There comes a time when the wind stops howling, the rain stops pouring, and the brilliance of a thousand rays of light beam down upon you. That is the time, my friend, when you finally made a discovery about yourself. By god, you've arrived! You did it and you love it. This is the moment when you erase all the pitfalls and draw in your own paradise.

What cruisers put on the line in order to achieve the ultimate dream is a true test of endurance. We walk our talk, take action, and risk everything to step aboard this life-altering journey sailing vessels to distant shores. Cutting the safety nets of society to chase distant horizons can be an exciting, soul-awakening adventure in life. When you not only survive this process, but thrive, you gain new insights about yourself. You become self-actualized, empowered.

The dues paid to enter *Cruising 101* will become the bargain of the century. Once underway, your cruising adventure will never cease, even if you find yourself back where you are sitting at this moment. How can that be? It is simple. The activity of cruising will transform into the philosophy of cruising.

Lessons learned in *Cruising 101* are lessons applicable to life. For us, this became clear at the end of our first cruise, when we returned to the States to prepare for our next journey.

We entered the other side under dark, smog-filled skies with the feeling of impending doom. A thousand green-backs and a beat-up Volkswagen Rabbit bandaged with the hope of a few more miles. Not much reassurance. Before we made our sojourn, we would have viewed this circumstance as one step short of being homeless.

There was no question about our survival, however. Limitations had been toppled like paper fences. Our cruising experience brought about the realization that our worst case scenarios in a metropolitan existence could never occur. When the going gets tough, the tough go to Mexico. Everything would go right for us, because we would make it happen.

Time passed, and we became embattled once again, side-by-side with the rest of society. Then a knock would come to the door. Standing large as life would be a reminder of what it, life, was really about. Working to live, rather than living to work.

These wonderful visitors from the past recant our own stories where we all played a part. They are the extended family we adopted from our journey. Uncle Dennis and Aunt Paula, from *Backstreets*, on the line telling us they are back on the mainland. Brother Mark, from *Puff*, who spent the holidays with us. Recently, cousins Norm, off *China Girl*, and Steve, off *I Did It*, stopped by for a reunion. They send their letters and their encouragement. They send their love.

What they send most is sanity. A wake-up call to remind us that our life is on hold until we return home, to the sea.

For some, cruising was not the paradise they had in mind. It may not be yours. But remember, you dared to do it. Knowing alternatives in life exist is half the battle. Now you no longer need to dream. You simply *do*.

Doing can be much simpler with a guide to pave the way. By removing the roadblocks and filling the potholes, your cruise can avoid some of the emotional and financial tolls others have hit on the way.

Preparation and the first 101 days of a cruise is the real test, the time frame that renders for most the pass-or-fail verdict. It is a period when high expectations, not curiosity, are what kill the cat.

Identifying the pitfalls is the road map to paradise. *Cruising 101* provides this guide by addressing the adventure of sailing off into the sunset, skewing the information toward the psyche, rather than the sails.

There isn't a cruiser we have met who was fully cognizant of the struggle and risks they would be forced to undertake, when their plans were merely on a conversational level. As we now look back on our dream, we can see that many mistakes and miscalculations could have been avoided, both prior to departure and beyond. During the thirty months spent preparing and acting on our goal, we have had the opportunity to talk to countless individuals and compare their experiences and miscalculations with our own. The similarities are not coincidental.

Little did we know of the tears that would be shed while engaging ourselves in what seemed to be such a positive endeavor. The starts and stops of our finances, emotions, and often our relationship, put our goal constantly at risk.

Of all those who have a vessel and a dream to someday go cruising, a microscopic percentage act on it. Of those who do, a high percentage turn back, often short of the time frame they had intended.

What happens to the dream that allows one to abandon it? Why are the first 101 days so crucial to the success of a major lifestyle change?

Of the dozens of books we have read, only a few touch on what we now consider the most important piece of equipment a dreamer-turned-doer can take aboard, a positive and flexible attitude. So often it is this single piece of equipment that will provide the solution when reality bangs on your hull.

What kind of information can two novice cruisers offer to help reduce the confusion? Not much if one is interested in someone with 50,000 miles under their keel. A lot if you are interested in seeing cruising from the perspective of folks just like you, who are still new enough at the game to remember the first lessons.

The first part of *Cruising 101* is an account of *Free Fall's* voyage south and the first few months of our new lifestyle as cruisers. These were troubled times for us, when we were constantly at risk of abandoning our goals. Our experiences may appear to be a calamity of sorts, but keep in mind that our stories have easily been topped by fellow cruisers.

More than one vessel has met its fate upon a rocky shoreline, but such losses can be overcome. Far greater risks are involved when a cruise goes badly for a couple, and the most tragic result is often the loss of each other. When a relationship disintegrates, so do the dreams and hopes for their tomorrows.

There is much to learn from our numerous mistakes made down the coast and beyond, but there is far more to be gained by how we and others overcame this time of turbulence and finally adjusted to our new way of life.

Part two of *Cruising 101* is dedicated to the lessons learned by those who went before you, and provides information to make your path easier to follow. Practical solutions are given which will keep you true to your course, along with your relationship and cruise.

Learn how to set attainable goals and realistic expectations, without risking your life savings or your motivation to go cruising. Find out how to grab the reins of an out-of-control budget and lead it to an affordable cruise, from purchasing and equipping your vessel, to living on a modest budget across the border.

An in-depth look at the cruising community and all the facets of its culture is provided. Take a quick course in cruising etiquette, and learn how to avoid offending your hosts in a foreign port.

A voice will finally be given to the unmentionables of cruising, which have left more than one baffled cruiser raining tears in his wake. *Cruising 101* will provide a process of identifying and overcoming the pitfalls and help you to recognize the paradise you will find as a reward for your efforts. ⚓

Dreams into Action

Jumping the Fence

...Until one is committed there is hesitancy,
the chance to draw back, always ineffectiveness.
—Murray

*C*ommitment. So much struggle and so much letting go, once this word sees action.

When we first considered cruising in a sailboat, we yearned for peace from city life and society's time schedule. We wanted more than just weekends to decompress from nine-to-five living. Carried deep within our hearts was a great urge to escape the corral which was fencing us into a life of mediocrity. Cruising became the solution.

The decision to go cruising released a thousand emotions, each surfacing to the top like steam in a kettle, ready to blow. We tumbled into a state of anticipation and optimism. We had a mission, and the world began to open up to us. Where did we want to go? What did we want to see? If the world was a book, we were just beginning to turn its pages. And in such a state of mind, it is not the endless horizon that poses limits, but oneself.

Perhaps we will be the first to tell you that cruising, from preparation through enactment, is not easy. Most escapes aren't. There is fear to overcome, some real, most imagined. There is work to do, for the mind, body, and soul. There is even a price tag, paradise is not free.

Although you quickly realize the power is yours when determining the price you are willing to pay. Some of your payment will be in dollars, but undoubtedly an emotional surcharge is included.

During our initial stages of cruising we stumbled into a few mountains. Thankfully, our miracles far outweighed those bumps. Our commitment was continually tested and we had to look toward each other for constant encouragement and resolve.

Some people shared our ambitions and fueled our intentions to sail off. Others were skeptical and could only offer water to pour on our fire. It is amazing how many people suggested we rent the film *Dead Calm*. Warnings of pirates with Uzis and whales with bad attitudes were common. A rare few shared our vision of fiery sunsets and lazy afternoons with time to cross borders and discover new ground, both in the world and within ourselves.

Those visions became nourishment for our dreams, and kept us inching along. But the closer we came to reaching our goals, the more complex and confusing the game of cruising became. Time was the last thing we had.

The moment we acquired *Free Fall*, our 30-foot Cal sloop, we were mentally ready to leave. Unfortunately, a mind-boggling amount of details needed attention prior to departure. Funding, boat modifications, education, liquidation; the list went on and on, and so did our considerations. As is the case with many fledging dreamers-turned-doers, we greatly underestimated the difficulty of our endeavor.

The day we bought the vehicle of our dreams, we allocated one year to prepare both our vessel and ourselves for departure. Our sights were initially set on the South Pacific, with hopes of completing a circumnavigation within our first year or two.

Almost every facet of the trip changed long before we left the slip. We made numerous miscalculations, suffering setbacks that constantly tested our resolve. Preparation and tying up loose ends took far more time and effort than first anticipated.

The target became Mexico after discovering the increase in costs and the tedious paperwork necessary for the South Pacific. French Polynesia holds bonds on visiting vessels. Food and fuel expenses inflate as soon as you "turn right." And a life raft would be necessary for a 2,500-mile crossing, yet another added expense. Unless we were willing to postpone the voyage, these demands could not be met in time.

Getting *Free Fall* seaworthy was more demanding than we expected, both mentally and financially. Although we purchased her for a more than fair price, we soon realized that if not careful, she could consume the entire cruising kitty. Every bolt, block, and shackle seemed to cost a small fortune. The rigging, electronics, and simple hardware put an immediate drain on our finances. Early on we began searching for ways to lower the boat's costs, taking shortcuts where we safely could.

It was fortunate we found some resourceful solutions to combat the costs, and were willing to take alternate routes to get where we needed to be. It was also fortunate that, as a couple, we buoyed each other's enthusiasm when one began to collapse under the weight of our ambitions. We were already on the path to discovering the power of flexibility and attitude management.

Through ingenuity, hard work, and the wisdom of a few knowledgeable friends, *Free Fall* became seaworthy, as did we.

One of those friends eventually joined our efforts and agreed to sign on as a temporary third crew member. He was to share in both the labor and the rewards of the trip south. An additional pair of eyes to keep watch for freighters, a strong pair of hands to help pull down sails and the shorter watch schedules during night sails were obvious advantages. The disadvantages were not so obvious.

The final countdown prior to our grand departure would start, stop, reschedule, and repeat in a vicious cycle, with the eventual letdown. Our third crew member had his own agenda and his own delays. Each delay was money spent to us. We were no longer employed, leaving behind the security of a weekly paycheck. Our day proved anticlimactic once it arrived. We had spent most of the night before working diligently, making last minute accommodations for scuba tanks, brought by our third crew member.

More than once, frustration boiled into anger and vaporized our enthusiasm. On these occasions, our mediocre, fenced-in lives would become appealing once more. Often our trip was at risk of cancellation when attitudes became inflexible and complicated.

Fortunately, we kept one foot stretched toward the line of freedom, with one fist wrapped tightly around victory. Providence may have delivered us to this line, but it was our commitment that made us cross.

We managed to overcome the details and fall free from the corral we once found ourselves trapped in.

Monday, March 21, 1994 we threw our stern to the wind and headed south, en route to our first destination: San Diego. ⚓

...a rhythm pulsed through Free Fall. And with Mexico beckoning across the border, the tempo stepped up a beat.

Our First Passage

The Rhythm's Gonna Get You

We are here and it is now. Further than that,
all human knowledge is moonshine.
—H.L. Mencken

𝒜 trip from Long Beach to San Diego was scheduled as our first. The short passage was expected to be pleasant and relaxed, but became one fouled by moody winds and stormy weather. Daysailing was fine, but once the sun dipped below the horizon, the frigid winds and stinging spray battered the crew. After making little progress, we sought refuge in Newport and again in Oceanside.

Thankfully, the trip from Oceanside to San Diego brought fair winds, calm seas, and a merciful sun.

Free Fall entered San Diego's harbor under a full moon. A star-lit canopy competed with the city lights for attention, surrounding us with a sense of being magically suspended. Our first passage was complete. The exhilaration we felt upon entering the harbor lingered for days.

After arriving, we began final preparations for Mexico. Although we had numerous projects and final provisioning to do, we were finally living a lifestyle that was but a dream only days before. The physical universe of our tiny sailboat was a hard reality, which brought new challenges.

Adapting to such limited space was the biggest obstacle (*Free Fall* has a two-foot wide walking corridor that extends a mere nine feet). Although there are numerous benefits to having the strength of three on board, new problems also arise. We were crammed together like too many coats in a closet. As such, temperaments often became wrinkled and needed to be ironed out.

Few amenities and no room for mistakes exist once the lines are cast and land is left behind. Everything needed for sustenance had to be stored in our 30-foot floating home—a thorough first-aid kit, a complete kitchen, spare parts and tools, water and fuel. The list goes on and on. Cruising lists usually do.

Despite the numerous last minute details prior to crossing the border, our sense of urgency had dissipated. The element of time had shifted, days blending together. With little need to keep track of dates, we set our own pace.

Time became associated with movement. From making breakfast and simple repairs, to moving on, a rhythm pulsed through *Free Fall*. And with Mexico beckoning across the border, the tempo stepped up a beat. ⚓

*It was easy to imagine
we were the first
to gaze toward those
untamed shores...*

Borderline

San Diego to Bahia Magdalena

It is good to have an end to journey toward;
but it is the journey that matters, in the end.
—Ursula K. Le Guin

We expected the sail from San Diego to La Paz to be the longest and most arduous stretch of the journey. But *Free Fall's* first major passage—cut short at Puerto Magdalena—was much more than we bargained for.

Leaving San Diego under sunny skies and light air, we sailed 80 miles off the coast to chase the wind and avoid heavy freighter traffic. The land melted beyond the horizon; the last we would see for days.

On our third day out, the wind speed noticeably increased. At that moment we were grateful. Although we had not managed to cover the 100-miles-a-day goal we had set, the wind finally appeared to be in our favor. With a fresh breeze blowing off her quarter, *Free Fall* made up for lost time. Our sails remained reefed, despite any extra speed possible running full sail. There was no race at this point, and we wanted to avoid any unnecessary stress on the sails and rigging. It proved a wise decision.

Once vessels leave the United States, it can be difficult to obtain accurate weather forecasts. We had acquired several up-to-date reports from our short-wave receiver, along with passing freighters. According to them, we had desirable conditions.

Unfortunately, the meteorologists were wrong. Although prepared and capable of handling a storm, it did not sit well with our vision of paradise. A storm at sea was a bit more of an adventure than we expected, or wanted.

The turbulence appeared without warning, dragging us away from a restless sleep. We stumbled out of the cabin to help our third crew member, who was on watch. The shock of cold spray was there to greet us. Winds up to 40 knots sent breaking seas smacking against our broadside, forcing a change in course out to sea.

The boom dangerously began a series of accidental jibes, due to erratic shifts of wind and confused seas. It was a cause for alarm, because of the damage that could be endured by the mighty swing of the boom.

Many sailboats have been demasted from this occur-rence, turning them into useless bathtubs within seconds. And more than one sailor has taken a knock to the head.

Water invaded our companion-way hatch when an uninvited wave swept over us at the same time coffee was being handed out. The bedding took most of the brunt, and our soggy habitat more than damp-ened our spirits.

The wildness of a storm can prove unnerving, and often leaves you feeling like a fly stuck to sticker-tape. Although the enraged sea had drawn us into this battle, we were the only ones concerned with its outcome. The sea cares for no one.

Our chariot *Free Fall* led us to safety, and this battle ended in victory. We crushed our fear, while maintaining the strictest control over the reins of destiny. The storm melted into oblivion. It was a moment of exhilaration.

After a drenched and sleepless night, the dawn brought on a welcome calm. Both the vessel and our expectations sustained a bit of damage, but *Free Fall* would touch Mexican shores.

Later, we realized we fared well compared to other vessels caught in the storm. One lost her spreaders and came close to demasting.

Our damages were fairly minor. The wind ripped out the radio's antenna, along with the masthead strobe light. A few of the fasteners holding the mainsail to the mast track had snapped and the tiller was cracked.

La Paz would have to wait. We needed to lick our wounds and make repairs. We were exhausted from our watch cycle—two hours on, four off. Certainly the rough ride down and the depletion of fresh food did nothing to improve our dispositions.

The wind was not cooperative once again. The dead calm and flat seas were welcomed for all of a single day. Impatience set in and we began bickering out of frustration and discomfort. The storm had forced a change in course, and we found ourselves 120 miles offshore. Fuel limitations restricted using the motor for any great distance and our water supply would not accommodate bathing for three people. The closest anchorage was only a day or so away, but our sails hung empty.

It was a lesson we were quickly grasping. When cruising, you must beach your time schedules, and go when the wind blows.

The winds finally did blow, and we approached Bahia Santa Maria, a small bay located just north of Magdalena Bay. It was like sailing into the production of a Walt Disney film. Dolphins and whales greeted us with great spouts of water. Huge kamikaze pelicans dove to the sea at uncanny speeds, erupting spray several feet into the air. The waters turned red where thousands of tiny pelagic crabs clung to each other, forming their own islands.

This was a land of isolation and delusion. It was easy to imagine we were the first humans to gaze toward those untamed shores, surrounded by claws of rock ripping up to the sky. When we neared the anchorage, however, we spied two boats bobbing off our bow.

We later discovered this entire area was renowned by naturalists worldwide. Local towns, like La Paz and Cabo San Lucas, provide tourists with an expensive pay-per-view of the bays and their popular seasonal guests—the grey whales. Each year the whales return to their birth grounds to give life to future generations.

The anchorage may be a haven for the whales, but its biting winds are less than welcoming to visiting vessels. After hooking our anchor in as tight as a tick to skin, we settled in. Despite the rocking and rolling throughout the night, we found the reprieve soothing. After the harrowing haul to Mexico, a complete night's sleep was long overdue. With the added comfort of a warm meal, our spirits soared.

Time was short and we had to make it up the Sea of Cortez before hurricane season began—less than a month away. Our 30-foot vessel began to feel more like a prison by the eighth day, rather than the ultimate freedom we had anticipated.

Early the next morning we headed toward Puerto San Carlos, the closest semblance of civilization in the Bay of Magdalena. Images of real showers and beef tacos danced in our heads as we headed for our first Mexican port-of-call. ⚓

The village is under the rule of two influences: Christianity and The Sea...

Where the Whales Sing

Bahia Magdalena

A journey is a person in itself; no two are alike. And all plans, safeguards, policing, and coercion is fruitless. We find after years of struggle that we do not take a trip; a trip takes us.
—John Steinbeck

The small port of San Carlos was just seventeen miles up Magdalena Bay, but early in the day fog set in and we were unable to safely pass through the bay's entrance.

We spent the night floating off the coast, maintaining a careful watch to avoid colliding with vessels obscured by the fog. Visibility vanished beneath the clutches of this grey beast. After a large fishing vessel came alarmingly close, we clung to our VHF radio, spotlight, and airhorn, until the sun devoured the fog.

Early the following morning, we entered the bay and headed toward the channel using our charts. We knew of the numerous sand shoals throughout the bay, and were taking necessary precautions. Using lead lines and a spotter for shallow water, we slowly searched for channel markings to no avail.

Whenever sailing off the beaten track in Mexico, sailors must be cautious. Most channels are poorly marked, if at all. Puerto San Carlos was an unexpected trip for *Free Fall*, and our charts for this area were vague at best.

The sudden scraping sound as *Free Fall* hit the bottom was grating to both the ear and the mind. We changed course, but could not locate an escape into deep water. Voices were angrily raised amidst the confusion. The inevitable moment came. The ship lurched as the keel became buried in sand. *Free Fall* was aground and a worse state of affairs could not be imagined.

After failed attempts to hail other vessels on our radio and the passing Mexican "pangas" (small, flat-bottomed, fiberglass versions of skiffs), we were forced to become our own solution. Anything with substantial weight was placed on the starboard side of the vessel, including the crew.

For what seemed like hours we found ourselves hanging off of *Free Fall's* rigging, just above the water's surface, like towels hung out to dry. An attempted rescue using our inflatable dinghy and anchor was botched after our crew member lost an oar. As we watched the oar float off into the distance, we decided to wait for the tide to rise. Luckily, it was a short wait. With the hanging weight, engine power, and a forgiving tide, our vessel broke free from her sandy captor. We had just christened *Free Fall's* bottom.

With just a few hours of daylight left and Puerto San Carlos out of reach, we changed course for the much smaller village of Puerto Magdalena, commonly known as Man-O-War Cove. Just as the sun tucked away, we entered the harbor and anchored near several other American vessels. This tiny fishing village is where we formally entered Mexico.

The tacos we had been craving were not available in the village, but we did get solar showers on deck with our renewed water supply. It was absolutely wonderful to rediscover simple pleasures like walking. A Coke never tasted better. To three smokers out of cigarettes and stranded on a rather stressful 30-foot island, the inexpensive Mexican smokes were a joy.

Puerto Magdalena proved to be the Mexico of our dreams. The tiny village settled upon this barren island is operated under the rule of two influences: Christianity and The Sea. The village's occupants take both seriously.

They harvest their living off the sea, fishing with nets dragged behind their yellow pangas or free-diving the ocean's chilled depths for abalone. Some of them set traps just offshore for lobster, selling their daily catch in Puerto San Carlos.

Homes painted in cheerful pastels of blue and yellow, were made of cinder blocks, tin, and wooden planks stripped from beach-wrecked vessels. Many of the simple constructions did not have running water or solid floors.

A single light bulb is usually used within each dwelling until the town's generator shuts down early in the evening. During our stay, however, the generator was waiting for repairs. The nights passed by with the solitary lighthouse blinking in the black shoreline of Man-O-War Cove.

Some of the homes we entered had little furniture, but each possessed a tiny stove to prepare their main staples of fish and strong, sweet coffee. The villagers proudly display their few possessions on the walls, whether it be a guitar or a blurred photograph. We had the impression they needed little more, for they were a self-reliant, hardy people. Their lives were rich with family, faith, and tradition and little else mattered.

During our stay in Magdalena, we met friendly and generous people. We befriended two fishermen who shared their catch and spent a few evenings with us on *Free Fall*. Although little actual communication went on—most of it through Spanish dictionaries—they seemed to enjoy our music and cooking. They took us out in their panga to show off their impressive engines. We were reminded of small-town teenagers and their cruising hot rods, much like where we grew up.

Unfortunately, we met with more misfortune before our stay was over. The morning after we celebrated Kevin's 42nd birthday, we discovered strong winds had blasted away our dinghy and outboard during the night. It was worse than losing a car in the States. We now had no way to reach the shore other than swimming and hitching rides from incoming pangas and fellow Americans.

With hopes of a fisherman locating the missing inflatable, we remained a few days, but it had become property of the sea. Without the use of a dinghy, our stay came to a close.

Cabo San Lucas, an expensive city by most people's standards, became our next destination despite our limited funds. With our anchor weighed, we motored out of the bay before setting sail.

Our experiences certainly did not appear to carry all the charm of a John Steinbeck novel, and we were unwilling to accept his observations as our own. Hitting a storm and getting grounded were certainly unwelcomed potholes on our road to paradise. The loss of our inflatable, however, represented a hefty toll on what we thought was a free road. And we were stressing.

We had not yet allowed ourselves to let the *trip* take us and sit back to relax. We still struggled to shape and police the journey into our own limited imaginations, schedules, and expectations of what should be, rather than accepting what was. ⚓

...our first real showers would have grown a forest across the thirsty Baja...

Land's End

Cabo San Lucas

It is not the same to talk of bulls as to be in the bullring.
—Spanish Proverb

Towering stone arches surrounded by glorious white beaches and postcard blue water greeted *Free Fall* as she entered the most expensive port in the Baja: Cabo San Lucas. The 35-hour journey from Magdalena Bay went without mishap. After a single day spent in the local marina, we anchored just outside the harbor.

Despite the excessive rates, the marina offered some impressive luxuries. We used the time wisely to juice up the batteries, clean the decks, and replenish the water supply. The volume of sweet, fresh water used in our first real showers since San Diego would have grown a forest across the thirsty Baja desert.

Once in town, it was impossible to not spend money. After cooking meals nonstop with canned and dried goods, we could not resist the fresh tortillas and cold cerveza. Although there were a few deals in town, most restaurants were off limits to us. Very little provisioning occurred in Cabo. With the exception of eggs and bread, the grocery stores were far too expensive. Sad-looking vegetables were evidently worth their weight in gold in these parts. Clearly our budget would evaporate if too much time was spent in Cabo, and the gods would soon test this theory.

It is hard to believe that just over a dozen years ago, Cabo San Lucas was a tiny fishing village very similar to Puerto Magdalena. Today it is one of the most lucrative resort towns in Mexico, constantly vying for the American dollar. The town is being built around the flock of tourists. Condos and discos sprout up like a Chia pet. Given time, it could easily evolve into a taco and tequila version of Las Vegas. Although attractive to our crewmate and others, it proved distasteful to us.

Everything we loved about the charming Puerto Magdalena village was found lacking in Cabo. It seemed there were more Americans than in Los Angeles. And many were exceptionally drunk while attempting sloppy versions of the Lambada. Even tattooed gangbangers vacationed in this pulsing party town.

We made an attempt to join in the fun on our first night in town, but it proved to be disastrous. After anchoring and being taxied to the beach, we ate our dinner and walked around town. Early that evening we became bored and wanted to return to *Free Fall*. It was then that we discovered panga taxis retire at five o'clock, and we began our long search for a ride. Hours later we decided to locate our vessel in the dark and simply swim out. We looked and looked, but could not locate her from the shore.

An immediate panic set in when we discovered our vessel was missing. Everything we owned was on her. Travelers checks. Clothing. Passports. Mental flashes of returning to the States like refugees, homeless, broke, and flipping burgers for a living entered our minds.

After fruitless attempts to get help, a national came to our aid and allowed us use of his radio. A single vessel responded to our distress call and used his radar in hopes of locating *Free Fall*.

The radar almost immediately located a vessel entering the harbor. At almost the same instant we too spotted that very vessel, and it was towing our miracle. *Free Fall* was back!

The very same winds that had stolen our dinghy the week before had become wickedly greedy. In cahoots with a strong current, the winds caused our anchor to drag into deep waters and *Free Fall* headed out to sea. She was four miles out before being rescued by a group of cruisers. Five people orchestrated the entire rescue and we are forever indebted to them.

It took time to recuperate from this scare that had sorely tested our confidence. Although we had heard several horror stories from other sailors, we could not help feeling like an evil spell had been cast over our entire journey, and worried about what fate may have in store for us around the next corner. We decided to spend some time to rejuvenate ourselves, despite the incentives to exit Cabo with all speed. Complications were caused both by the loss of our inflatable and our nerve for anchoring. Regrettably, we moved to an expensive slip inside the marina.

Over a week later, we found our replacement dinghy; an ugly department store special. It resembled a giant grey donut, but didn't row nearly as well. With our new addition, *Free Fall* was ready to go once more and we put Cabo's arches to our stern, or so we thought.

Before continuing on to La Paz, we planned an overnight stop in a tiny anchorage called Santa Maria. Our overnight stop turned into a few pleasurable days snorkeling in the little horseshoe-shaped cove. There we caught the first fish of the voyage, and it seemed our luck was changing. But the moment we left the cove we were hit by the "washing machine", an erratic wave action caused by the Sea of Cortez meeting the Pacific. A storm also appeared to be in the immediate future of *Free Fall*, and we were forced to return to the land's end. Back into the den of the money-eating lion. ⚓

One Step Forward,
Two Steps Back

Return to Cabo

*A ship is safe in harbor -
but that is not what ships are built for.*
—John A. Shedd

Since the time we cut the lines, we have been counseling ourselves away from set deadlines and structured lives. Perhaps this is against the very grain of human nature. Maybe this mind-set simply needs to be cured like a bad habit.

Naturally, every plan must have a time boundary. In San Diego, we gave ourselves 15 days to reach La Paz, but we forgot about the lunch stops.

Thirty days into our voyage, with La Paz only 140 miles away, we were still in Cabo San Lucas. Certainly we were waiting for an opportunity to escape, one with better sailing conditions. But conflicts were rapidly developing on board between members of the crew. Those issues needed to be handled prior to leaving Cabo. There was the added element of getting stuck in one place, and some locations seem to stick to you better than bad credit.

Perhaps the greatest asset we possess as human beings is our ability to adapt. We can walk into almost any strange land, grab a beer and kick our feet up to watch the ongoing games. Within days we know our neighbors, the rules, and are gossiping like old sisters.

A foreign port becomes familiar within days. A local coffee shop turns into the morning watering hole. Before long, we are on a first name basis with the staff and have been treated to a flood of baby pictures.

Comrade cruisers we met in San Diego are greeted as old friends in Cabo. Invitations to dinners and snorkeling excursions are frequent. The next destination ultimately becomes delayed. And these delays have consequences on an established agenda, and are usually paid in full with both emotional and financial stress.

Our third crew member was not anxious to leave Cabo. He was in the middle of researching the possibility of starting a small business. Being single, he also enjoyed the social aspects of a city filled with vacationing American women. His adventure south was a short-term investment, so his financial considerations were not as restricting as ours. We, on the other hand, were desperate to reach La Paz. Cabo was expensive and our budget demanded a quick exit. A compromise was reached. We left too late and he left too early. Nobody on *Free Fall* left satisfied.

Our second run from Cabo was a success. This time we escaped the dreaded washing machine and motored to Los Frailes, officially entering the Sea of Cortez. After spending the night anchored, we sailed north toward the higher latitudes.

It was like entering a land from a prehistoric time, which refused to succumb to civilization. A heavy fog distorted the rocky, barren landscape, playing tricks with our eyes throughout the day. Both the shoreline and the sea's numerous islands appeared to float above the waterline.

Hardly a trace of man's existence could be found. A rare vessel occasionally would be spotted off in the distant haze. According to the charts, a few tiny fishing villages were nestled somewhere on shore. But they were erased from sight by the suspended white mist. We finally took our cue from the magical Baja surroundings and let our spirits soar.

As we evaluated our trip down the coast, we realized how misguided we had been. Certainly we had been tested, and made some errors with devastating effects. Unfortunately, we had focused only on the negative, completely losing sight of the positive.

When just off of Magdalena Bay, a pair of pilot whales passed our bow and swam into the most marvelous sunset we have ever seen. So powerfully beautiful, the image stopped us from moving. And though no photograph was taken, the memory burned itself into our hearts.

Countless pleasant evenings were spent drinking coffee and playing the guitar under the weight of a million stars. Suffice it to say, there wasn't a lack of beauty on the trip.

People have befriended us at every port. Even in Cabo San Lucas, friends emerged from the drunken masses to lift us back on our feet.

Traveling about in a sailboat involves a great deal of work, and it has as many obstacles as any other environment. But during such emotional highs, the rewards seem endless.

One evening we found ourselves anchored off Isla Cerralvo. A playful band of dolphins came to visit and set a festive spell. We spent a few pleasant hours casting a line into the sparkling waters. Although the fish declined our bait, we did catch a glorious sunset, sharing its pastels with the sea below.

As delightful as this area was, it could only be credited with part of our good spirits. After a string of delays, blunders and mishaps, *Free Fall* was close to the first major triumph of the journey.

Although destinations originally were not supposed to have such an impact, La Paz had mentally become our pass-or-fail verdict. We were certainly evolving into cruisers, but we had yet to reach our first planned port-of-call. The dangling carrot was a mere 25 miles away.

Looking back on the journey down the Pacific, we should have taken more planned lunch stops. Somehow we had become involved in a race, quite like the ones we entered daily on the freeways we left back home. It took a while to learn to avoid the population centers like Cabo, and spend more time in places like Magdalena Bay and Isla Cerralvo. Often the quieter places off the beaten track carry some exceptionally fine dining for the mind and spirit, with very affordable prices. ⚓

*We made an
evening ritual of
watching the brilliant
sunsets from a bench
overlooking the sea...*

The City Of Peace

La Paz

They sail down here from way up north, with tales of ocean lore.
Impressing all the local folk, who've heard it all before.
—Kevin Donnelly

On a simmering day with strong north winds filling our sails, we entered La Paz sailing the same route pirates had once used to raid the city hundreds of years ago. We too came to plunder some of the rich bounty the old port had to offer. Its sunsets are world renowned, and some of its ice cream parlors ought to be. During a three week stay we had our fill of both.

La Paz is one of the largest metropolitan locations in the Baja peninsula, and has both the conveniences and afflictions of most modern cities. Today one can find just about anything in La Paz. Reeboks, fancy colognes, and most marine items are all quickly accessible. Like most cities, they have huge air-conditioned department stores, banks, restaurants, and hotels. There is an airport and dozens of taxis compete for the limited clientele. La Paz could even boast about its daily traffic jams and graffiti, if a city was to be flattered by such things.

There are some startling differences in La Paz when compared to American cities, however. For such a beautiful and historically colorful city, it still lacks a sufficient sewage system. On the waterfront, the cement path crumbles into the sea, offering starry-eyed lovers an opportunity for broken legs. Much of the construction seemed to be built for only tomorrow's use, with little hope that any of the newer buildings would see the next decade.

A few of Mexico's deals whispered to us long before we left California were finally discovered after tremendous stone turning. We had a full course dinner, along with drinks, for under five dollars. The nameless joint would certainly not meet any type of health regulation, but the family who ran it fried some excellent chicken.

On the waterfront, next to a giant palm tree painted white with gay colored circles, we found one of the last remaining pearls of La Paz. The pleasant little parlor by the beach was called La Fuente, and its specialty was homemade ice cream. They had ice cream and sherbets made out of exotic ingredients, some unknown to us. There were flavors of apple and coconut, watermelon and banana. For the entire stay we made an attempt to sample each flavor on one of their huge sugar cones. We made an evening ritual of watching the brilliant sunsets from a bench overlooking the sea while savoring the icy treats.

Although many great bargains still remain in Mexico, most of them require a lengthy search in the tourist centers. Gone is the age of five-dollar lobster dinners and ten-dollar hotel stays. However, ten bucks for a lobster dinner is still a deal, and one of many which continually tested our resolve in the big tourist towns of the Baja.

These little temptations quickly added up financially and posed a threat toward our limited cruising funds. One lesson gained from our experiences in both Cabo and La Paz was to either limit our stay in cities or avoid them altogether. ⚓

*Not only did we catch
some excellent tasting
fish, but we also caught
some captivating sights
of the Baja Sur.*

Two Live Crew

Reaching the Crossroads

Life can only be understood backwards;
but it must be lived forwards.
—Søren Kierkegaard

*I*t was once said that the only constant in life is change, and despite this great truth, no manual was left as a guide to cope with the details left in the wake of change.

We both knew our third crew member was searching for something located in a direction opposed to ours. He was with us on a short leave of absence from society and would soon be returning. The crossroad had been reached. The three of us learned hard lessons during the first two months, and none of us wished to continue the voyage together, despite the many positive experiences we had shared.

Three is literally a crowd for the limited space of a 30-foot vessel, particularly for long-term arrangements. A couple joining up with a third party seems to be brewing up a recipe for mutual discontent. There was no privacy available, and we were forced to learn about each others' idiosyncrasies while attempting to deal with them.

By the time we reached La Paz, our friendship was held together by a tattered thread. We had conflicting agendas and only one could be met. Our crewman formally made the break by agreeing to "boat sit" another cruiser's vessel, leaving us to pick up the pieces. Our own relationship had become as fouled as the weather we hit on the way down, and we needed to make some serious repairs. His decision was met with relief, from all parties.

Throughout our voyage we encountered several abandoned vessels left to rot in the sea. The skeletons were the haunting reminders of broken dreams and relationships. Many were left by couples who likely carried our same aspirations and commitment. We couldn't imagine leaving *Free Fall* in a makeshift grave in some anchorage, with no life or love remaining on her. So we pushed through this period. We left La Paz as well as many of the troubles and tribulations since our journey had begun.

The real cruising, or the real fun of cruising, had begun. No more Pacific swells. No more night sails. No more arguing. It was back to being a partnership, one joined by the single mission of loving our surroundings and each other.

Because it was just the two of us, we were understandably nervous as we left La Paz. We had to adapt to not having a third crewman there, to share the responsibilities, the occasional chaos, and certainly a fair portion of fault.

Free Fall sailed north on a course toward Puerto Escondido, located about 120 miles up the coast. We chose the remote "hidden harbor" as our next port-of-call for numerous reasons, the most serious being the start of the hurricane season.

Not only is Escondido the best hurricane hole in the Baja, but there are numerous isolated islands just outside the harbor that can be reached within hours. Hurricanes in this part of the world are observed as closely as a difficult pregnancy. There is plenty of warning which enables alert cruisers to race back from the islands to the safety of the harbor.

One other personal incentive drew us to Escondido. A couple that had become both friends and mentors was waiting for us to arrive before they continued north on their own journey. They had been dockmates of ours in Long Beach. These experienced cruisers began their second Mexico cruise months before us, but in their wake they left gifts of knowledge and inspiration.

Our friends could not wait long for us, but we had enough time to make a few stops along the way. It would be some time before we could safely go south again, so we sucked up the sights and made notes of the places we would visit again.

Ensenada Grande, a large cove located on Isla Partida was our first brief stop. The beautiful white beaches piled high with exotic shells and surrounded by inviting blue waters was impossible to resist. We spent a full day exploring the beaches and snorkeling in the crystal clear waters, mesmerized by the flashing display of tropical fish. This is the place where we began our Baja shell collection, which now threatens to overflow our limited space.

Two days later and further up the Baja coast, we spent the night anchored off San Evaristo, where a tiny fishing camp is located. When we arrived, the fishermen's siesta was in full swing.

The siestas we had viewed so far were much more than an afternoon shuteye. The tradition seemed to include a heavy flow of cerveza and tequila, with intermediate napping right on the beach. Part of the day's celebration was for their great catch of fish earlier in the day.

Other than a few small fish that would barely make a taco, our fishing luck was nil. There must be some great knowledge, some hidden secret passed down in the generations of fisherman, of which out-siders are kept ignorant.

In Bahia Agua Verde, our final and most satisfy-ing stop before Escondido, our luck changed. Not only did we catch some excellent tasting fish, but we also caught some captivating sights of the Baja Sur. A small isolated village overlooking the bay added to the area's charm.

In the village there is a tiny store filled with only dry goods and a single room family planning center, about the size of a tool shed. The town boasts a restaurant, where one must make reservations early in the day. The owner/manager/cook must prepare his living room for the guests, where they will dine on the single item on his menu: fish tacos with beans.

Somewhat reluctantly, we left the peaceful Agua Verde, along with its people and dazzling sunsets.

On our short trip to Puerto Escondido, the sun shining on the little village must have radiated its joy onto *Free Fall*. As soon as we left the bay, a kind wind picked us up and dropped us off, providing one of our most delightful sails ever. ⚓

What appeared to be a loud and hectic RV campground became Free Fall's home for many months...

Gypsy Hook

The Hidden Harbor

With masts like cuts across the sky, behind a setting sun;
joined with common sutured thoughts of what they have begun.
—Kevin Donnelly

Towering, craggy mountains posed a formidable background on the western side of the huge anchorage, where over a hundred vessels rested. The buzz of activity was simply astounding. It certainly wasn't what we had expected before we headed *Free Fall's* bow into Puerto Escondido, known as the Hidden Harbor.

People were doing their laundry, hanging it out on the lines of their vessels. Some folks were on deck having cocktails, while others were in the cool waters shaking off the mid-day heat. The whining drone of engines from small inflatables were heard before their owners flashed by like mosquitoes aimed to a light.

What appeared to be a very loud and hectic RV campground turned out to be *Free Fall's* home for many months. Perhaps it was the magical evenings that hypnotized us into staying. Certainly the wonderful islands beckoning us just miles from our little harbor added to the magic. The happily-ever-after, however, took some time to achieve as we began to adjust to our new lifestyle.

There is far more to being a cruiser than simply owning a boat and relocating to a foreign port. The cruising community has its own culture, with its own rhyme and reason. Learning the rules of the road, and settling into this admittedly tight community is no easy task.

Although Escondido was packed with other cruisers, no ceremonial welcome mat was provided by the community. Once our former dockmates continued their journey north, our initial delight of reaching Escondido quickly dwindled. Some members of this community had been cruising since the seventies, and had seen green folks like us come and go daily. They had long since overcome the newness of passage making, and were already well adapted to living on a boat in foreign waters.

Most of these seasoned cruisers had little or no interest in becoming involved with newcomers. All the stories told about the harrowing trips south had been heard before. The continual flow of questions on the morning net was as repetitive as the wail of sirens in the cities we had left behind.

We began to learn about and relate to the new community we had joined.

It took us some time to leave any emotional wreckage in the past, and settle into the rhythm of our new surroundings. The constant struggle to allow both our dreams and relationship to survive stormed throughout the first month of hurricane season. The ups and downs of adjusting to a completely new lifestyle were at times exhausting.

We eventually overcame and began to thrive, but the process of feeling at peace with our new environment and our new selves was not an overnight event. Indeed, months later we had both changed considerably. And just like seeds lying dormant throughout a harrowing winter, we eventually flowered under the brilliance of the sun and the warmth of friends. Our confidence grew, where it once floundered.

No longer was it a question as to whether we made the right decision to act on our dream. ⚓

*By focusing on
the trials of the trip,
we forgot about our
hard-earned victories.
We had lost sight of our
forest through the trees...*

Chapter 1
Attitudes, Goals
and Expectations

How to Eat the Elephant

There is a certain relief in change, even though it be from bad to worse; as I have found in traveling in a stage coach, that it is often a comfort to shift one's position and be bruised in a new place.
—Washington Irving

One Year Later

𝐴n abrupt change in *Free Fall's* motion awakened me from a state of suspended animation to one of total awareness. The steady snap of flags flailing against the rigging underlined the urgency in my mind.

Amy was already out the companion-way hatch as I bounded up the two short steps to the cockpit. The harbor, etched over the eons into the rocky shoreline of Mexico's Baja coast, had once again transformed itself. Puerto Escondido no longer was a pond that would allow us to view the cosmos looking either up or down. Instead, it was the reality check all cruisers confront when the north winds begin to howl.

After a quick check to confirm we were holding and a glance to make sure our dinghy was still attached to its painter, we began the ritual of checking the 40 other anchor lights, flailing violently throughout the harbor. Once assured that none of our neighboring vessels were dragging down on us, we went below and prepared a fresh pot of coffee. It was 3:35 a.m.

We were just shy of 14 months since leaving our Long Beach Marina slip. As we began to evaluate our current situation, our conversation drifted to the countless experiences and the wealth of information we had gathered.

How fortunate we considered ourselves. We had, thus far, succeeded where many had run aground. The onset of 30-knot winds through an anchorage no longer spooked us, nor were we confused by the customs and etiquette surrounding a cruising fleet. Life had become merely the details of living afloat in paradise. We had survived the long list of anticipations and expectations, incidents and accidents, only to adapt to what had become the actuality of Cruising 101.

The game, we now concluded, was won or lost on attitude and flexibility, not the control we tried to exert over details that would not conform to the expectations we once held. More often than not, it was how we chose to see our events that had the most profound effect on our outlook. By simply learning to be flexible in looking at situations, many potential problems began to dissolve with little or no action required.

In the effort to remain students of our new lifestyle, we began to observe a pattern of common mistakes, not only in our own actions, but also of the others we met during our first year out. Few of us predicted the impact of a total lifestyle make-over and the confusion that comes along for the ride.

Setting virtually unattainable goals and then attaching them to unrealistic expectations is one of the initial mistakes common to most aspiring cruisers. Of the fellow dreamers-turned-doers we have met, many like us set their sights on long-term circumnavigations.

It should have seemed obvious to those of us who have dreamed of sailing around the world that it would require some time to adapt to a very different lifestyle. Stateside decompression is not only a normal phase, but a required one for a successful cruising experience. Stepping out from a world controlled by daily planners and pagers into one where there is often no awareness of the date can be confusing. It took some time before we caught our collective breath and slowed down our pace.

We discovered the flaw in our grand expectations as we began to confront our new environment. There was a considerable gap between the dream and the reality. Dark clouds exist even in paradise.

Contrary to popular belief, sailing expertise and equipment on board is not a guarantee for a successful cruising adventure. Although seamanship is a very important aspect that cannot safely be ignored, it only provides one side of the equation for surviving the cruising lifestyle. Unfortunately, many are too late in this realization and are unable to salvage their dream. Tragically, many give up and return to the States, just steps short of reaching the shores of success.

Of the cruisers who turned back, many abandoned their quest because they were unable to adjust to reality when it did not match up to their expectations. Anyone who has been to La Paz, Mexico can confirm the evidence and availability of another's dashed dream just by counting the For-Sale signs. It was a miracle we were able to find the energy needed to rebound from some of our reality checks and their consequences. Flexibility became mandatory in order to adjust our expectations.

Attitude malfunction is seldom taken into account during the planning and pre-departure stages and few are prepared for the impact it has on the shakedown leg of the voyage and the first 101 days underway.

Few cruisers who left with plans to circumnavigate the globe do so, at least not in their first year out. Considering the statistics, this first major pitfall can be avoided by simply planning your first extended cruise as a shakedown, one that will determine if you even like the lifestyle. It is always best to put your toe in the water before jumping in.

By choosing a relatively local cruising ground and setting a realistic time frame to learn and adjust, you can stack the deck in favor of success. The impact of inevitable emotional hits during the early phase of a voyage will be reduced by a wide margin. When reviewing this approach in hindsight, we now realize how many options were available.

Using Mexico's Sea of Cortez as an example, a plethora of approaches exist to test the waters of cruising. Had we set our original goal as a learning excursion to Mexico, we would have felt far more successful when we arrived over a year ago. Adjusting to what we thought was a mandatory compromise in lieu of sailing the globe expended much of our attitude and energy.

The key is to break down the big dream into a series of small goals. Once achieved, put a notch in your belt and consider these to be successful accomplishments. As many cruisers have discovered during their first three months, the effort required to keep a positive outlook is overwhelming, especially when the big picture becomes the *only* picture.

Fatigue had taken its toll after our arduous trip down the Pacific Coast of Baja, Mexico. Adverse weather, insomnia, and the loss of equipment left in its wake a disgruntled crew. La Paz, for us, held few good memories based on our attitude and state of affairs. Our expectations were crushed by the time we had arrived.

Any burning desire to circumnavigate the globe was completely smothered, along with the enthusiasm we may have felt visiting this ancient city for the first time. Our mistake was to see this city as a compromise. This was the port where we had to confront the unrealistic goals and expectations we had set for ourselves. So heavy was our disappointment, at one point we nearly abandoned our commitment to the cruising lifestyle. By focusing on the trials and tribulations of the trip, we forgot about our hard-earned victories. We had lost sight of our forest through the trees that stood in our way.

A cloud of negativity crept on board, affecting our outlook as we plodded ahead. Our emotions spun like a child's Yo-Yo, reacting to every yank of the string life had to offer. The constant emotional highs and lows we experienced during our first few months of cruising left us completely drained.

The frustration and emotional exhaustion had a devastating impact. While anchored off a small island near Puerto Escondido, we discussed returning to the States. Our limits of endurance and frustration had been reached. To put it bluntly, our attitudes were in the toilet.

It was at that moment some cruising friends hailed us on the VHF radio and invited us to an anchorage a few miles north of where we had secluded ourselves. To this day we do not know why we pulled the hook and set sail.

What we do know is that our spontaneous decision turned out to be the turning point of how we saw our cruising experience. We realized others had experienced emotional turmoil during their adjustment to a very new way of life. Some recounted mistakes that made ours pale by comparison. The real breakthrough was the realization that everyone around us had succeeded. Most of our friends had begun their journeys months ahead of us and had already adjusted to the pitfalls we had yet to identify.

The page had finally turned and our emotions stabilized. It was a momentous step forward. This transformation occurred at the start of our fourth month out; a common time frame when freshmen cruisers adapt to their new lifestyle.

Many find the first few months of their cruise the most challenging. If you survive this three month transition, you are likely to continue the experience and view it as a success.

It now seems that with the passage of time and the adjustment it allows, most of our pre- and post-departure expectations, either positive or negative, were exploded when replaced by the reality of cruising. It has been our own hands-on observation that the worst case scenarios never occurred and the good experiences, once we had adjusted to the lifestyle, were better than we had ever expected.

The confusion, however, of having magical days like the ones experienced on our passage up from La

Paz to Escondido, followed immediately by devastating emotional lows shortly after we arrived at the Hidden Harbor was typical during the first three months. This emotional roller coaster can derail even the best laid plans. Hindsight has now taught us that you do not have to go through such a stressful ordeal.

Reflecting on all the things we could have done to smooth the transition, at the top of the list is a healthier respect for one of the few guarantees you can count on while cruising: a complete change of lifestyle.

An unidentified pitfall for many is the impact of a lifestyle devoid of stateside distractions and conveniences. Hot showers and a dependable telephone service are examples that come to mind, but joining us on a trip to town could help illustrate the frustration you may encounter in everyday living.

You have spent the morning searching for a ride into town to make an exchange for pesos at the bank. After managing to locate a ride, shared by a number of others in a quest for provisions and fuel, you squeeze in and hold your breath.

Upon arrival you exhale and cautiously exit the vehicle, newly shaped and plastered with sweat. Now, you already know the rule—no pesos exchanged after noon—so you rush off to join the line of customers flooding into the bank.

Five minutes to noon you reach the counter, blurting out your modest request to exchange a hundred dollars into pesos. The teller makes an announcement. She is sorry, but the bank has run out of pesos. Could you please come back tomorrow?

Certainly you have no choice but to crawl back empty handed into that sardine-can-on-wheels and wait for another day. But you do have a choice to either laugh or cry at the situation. We find that laughs are a lot more fun than tears.

Besides dealing with a country which is less concerned with dollar-producing efficiency and speed than our own, you also have to adapt to living without those stateside diversions.

Some cruisers are totally unprepared for the lack of artificial entertainment. It is so easy to pick up a newspaper or turn on the television when confronted with boredom in the States. Many take for granted the ability to jump in the car and head for the local pub or theater.

Here is a land where malls don't exist, nor do 24-hour grocery stores. Few of us in the States ever have to contend with all-day excursions to pick up a five-gallon jug of fuel and some essential provisions. When was the last time you had to haul water, just to do the laundry and take showers?

The lack of stateside conveniences and mind-numbing distractions is a bridge that must be crossed. By weaning ourselves away from the technological advances we are accustomed to, we become self-sufficient. Bouncing back technologically to the turn of the century has more emotional impact than many care to acknowledge, much less cope with.

Few of us are prepared for the role changes necessary for the inconvenient, time-consuming chores associated with life afloat. It is not possible for one person to be responsible for only those chores they tended to back in the States. It is so easy to see only the romantic side of sailing to foreign ports. Unfortunately, this miscalculation has been the downfall of many.

Is it all about inconvenience and hardship? Of course not. The same hardships we have addressed are the fuel for adjustment and the incredible enjoyment one can find in the simplicity of the cruising lifestyle. The point is that the transition, like a piece of coal, takes time before you ever see the diamond. By accepting the fact that a learning curve is mandatory, you will expect and accept the challenges of adjusting your lifestyle. Becoming aware of this transition will also make any inherent difficulties part of the price you are willing to pay for tuition. Call it paying your dues, if you like.

By embracing this challenge of adapting to a new way of living, you can begin to chart your progress and see the transition from a positive perspective, rather than an additional mountain standing in the path of your dream. The key to getting through the first 101 days is to be able to measure and feel some success to balance the confusion that is at the core of any emotional lows.

In order to stack the odds in your favor you must give yourself a series of goals attainable from the onset. For those who have not purchased their world cruiser, or even for those who have, the learning excursion philosophy will save you thousands of dollars and countless disappointments. Both a realistic time frame and a local cruising area greatly reduces the amount of money and effort needed to begin your adventure, not to mention providing a wide margin for error.

So why Mexico? For us it was local, convenient, and user friendly, as are many cruising grounds neighboring the United States.

For students of the cruising lifestyle, all the elements necessary to pass Cruising 101 are inherent. Navigating is coastal for the most part. The amount of equipment needed is minimal and can be added with little inconvenience. The cost of your cruising vessel can be greatly reduced and all the activities and beauty associated with cruising can be found at your own back door. It will also provide all the experience you will need, should you decide to extend the experience.

The succeeding chapters will assist you in flattening the learning curve with specific ideas and information as it pertains to the lifestyle adjustment. Before we do, however, it is important to touch on ways for you and your partner to increase your chances for success. ⚓

*"Above and beyond
all things you may do,
remember to be kind
to each other."*

Chapter 2
Relationships

Finding True Romance in a Broom Closet

After all, when you come right down to it, how many people speak the same language even when they speak the same language?
—Russell Hoban

*I*t's true! Where we have been cruising, dolphins dance upon our wake and manta rays glide above the surface of this prehistoric wonderland. Once settled into the lifestyle, sharing the magic with each other enhanced the quality of our experience.

Under a brilliant canopy of stars, we found ourselves discussing joint experiences and planning new ones. The environment for communication, while nestled in a remote anchorage or running under light wind, has a magic that rekindles the excitement felt in many a newfound romance.

Just as true is the intensity of emotion that can cause tempers to flair over seemingly minor disputes. Intense quarrels emanating from a neighboring vessel have disrupted the tranquility of more than one evening. Some of those disruptions were our own.

No greater tragedy exists than the dissolution of a cruising couple's dream when flare-ups escalate to the point of separation. Living in the confines of a sailboat, even a large one, is often a case study testing the limits of an individual and couple's tolerance. This occurs even in the best of relationships.

Contrary to the romance people link to the closeness of living aboard, your relationship differences will be magnified while underway or at anchor. Overestimating your ability, or that of your partner, to adjust to cramped quarters is a lesson that will become apparent the minute the shoreline fades into the distance.

If your relationship problems are obvious, we would strongly suggest you handle those issues on land. Besides the emotional upheaval you could well avoid, the very real component of safety must be considered. When caught in an angry ocean with 40-knots off the stern, it is not prudent to address what happened at a party five years back.

Open and honest discussion prior to leaving may help diffuse a time bomb once the trip is underway. Amy, for instance, was excited about our plan to go cruising from the start and therefore quite amazed at the number of women she met who were only along for the ride. I, on the other hand, was not surprised by the number of men who discovered their companions were not enjoying the dream. So often it was apparent that the lifestyle was not the paradise promised to the malcontent shipmate.

Asking some questions and hearing the answers is the first step to placing the odds in your favor. It is almost a prerequisite that you and your cruising partner determine that you are both singing from the same hymn book. To do anything less is to flirt with failure. In fact, it is most important when discussing your cruising plans to turn off your selective hearing apparatus. You and your co-adventurer must be very clear on what is being said and felt by each other.

Try these discussions on for size and begin to purge the pits in your paradise.

- Have you considered, honestly, that your dream may in fact be your partner's nightmare?

- Have you determined that their fears of leaving a secure environment cannot be overcome with knowledge and experience? If this is the case with you and yours, we suggest you cut your losses. To try and proceed with your plans and continue to have a relationship is akin to clawing off a lee shore without sails or engine.

- Have you painted only the positive side of the program when selling your significant other on the merits of cruising? Identifying some of the pitfalls is as important as talking about the positive aspects of sailing off toward the sunset.

- Is your partner aware of how important this dream is for you and are there other options open, especially if your companion is not enthused about the passage part of the program? Many couples handle this by the "fly in" method. One of the partners flies in to meet the vessel, once it has arrived in a designated port.

- Are you willing to do another's dream, in order to have them participate in yours? What if the other's dream was a big house in the country so the in-laws could have more room when they stop by to visit?

- Assuming your shipmate shares the dream, have you both sat down and discussed each other's reasons for sailing off and the individual goals and expectations held? A great method for this exchange of viewpoints is in the form of a letter, sent to the other individual. It provides a great platform to build on, if you focus first on expectations and desires you both hold in common.

- Is your decision to go cruising attached to hopes that you can resolve reoccurring issues between you and your partner? One of the most serious mistakes and a surefire road to disaster is when part of a couple's reason to go cruising is done with hopes that it will repair a shaky relationship. In every case we encountered, couples who have tried to use cruising as a form of "relationship therapy," have ended their trip abruptly, along with any hopes they had of working things out.

There are many other areas of discussion you will find yourselves engaged in as you gear up for D-Day (departure, not divorce). There is no doubt in our minds that those couples who were willing to prepare their heart and soul for the experience of a lifetime have also begun to shape an attitude they can call upon when all else fails.

For some unexplained reason, a stowaway named Murphy rides on board all vessels sailing off toward paradise. Even the most balanced of couples find themselves unnerved by his antics. What can go wrong will, be it equipment failure or the promise of fair weather, as you are pounding into sloppy seas from the direction you want to go. These examples are what we refer to as In-Your-Face dilemmas. They are the uncontrollable predicaments that often have a severe impact on attitudes and relationships.

Other not so obvious but still considered In-Your-Face situations include tropical heat, seasickness, or maybe something as trivial as misplacing a novel two pages short of finding out whodunnit.

A classic example on *Free Fall* was what we fondly call The Head Incident. It was when our head broke, and sure enough, we lost our heads. We were expecting guests from the States on the 5 p.m. flight to Loreto. Low and behold, when the toilet was flushed, the pump handle came off. Needless to say we had in our midst an In-Your-Face problem, not to mention an In-Your-Nose problem.

Thank God, over the year we had been cruising we learned to develop some sense of irony and humor. Not something found too readily during the first three months of cruising.

Dear friends of ours who seemed to have Murphy and his extended family on board provided a source of learning and inspiration. We couldn't help but be inspired at the way these folks dealt with uncontrollables. Even after a lightning bolt exploded their masthead antenna, this crew began repairing the problem without the slightest hint of ill-tempered moods or the "why us" syndrome. Humor was even present when one of them commented, while looking at their masthead with binoculars, that the antenna resembled a bouquet of stems, minus the flowers.

Perhaps the best defense for the havoc Murphy reaps is the power of humor. It allows one to act, rather than react. How a cruising couple decides to handle Murphy is often determined by the way they see their roles prior to departure.

Traditional roles shift as the cruising experience unfolds. A not uncommon phenomena while cruising is the personality change that may become evident in the less dominant member of the crew.

Couples who have spent time honing their communication skills will arrive at the end of this transition with a solid working relationship. We have met many who are well adjusted to the diversified roles that cruising will demand from its participants. There are women we know who have taken on the responsibility of their vessel's diesel, while their spouses assume the shopping and cooking chores.

In our particular case, Amy is the hunter when it comes to catching food from the sea, while I now do a chore I have always detested, dish washing. Life aboard a cruising vessel demands teamwork. There is just too much that must be done to simply divide it up along traditional gender roles, not that there are any left as we head toward the 21st century. Hauling water, fuel, and supplies, along with housekeeping and general boat maintenance calls for the strength of two.

In the absence of modern appliances, laundry and dishes must be done by hand. Although this may sound like a dreadful way to escape to paradise, the fact is, accomplishments are truly the mutual possession of the couples involved.

Those who were quiet and agreeable can become assertive and independent once they begin to acquire new talents. For couples willing to allow for this process of growth, the effects are usually positive. Still, the adjustment and transition can throw confusion into the lap of the partner who is forced to accept the change.

Decisions necessary when cruising will frequently involve the health and welfare of any recipient of that decision. It is only human for another to interject if they feel jeopardized by the action of the captain responsible for their well-being. Those who were accustomed to allowing another to make decisions for them on land may not be inclined to do so at sea. We are emphatic about the need to address this issue prior to heading out.

If you have found a sense of mutual excitement with the concept of cruising, you must include some discussion on how to handle the captaincy of your vessel. Although gender is not an issue—we have met several female captains—someone must be in command and another must be willing to agree when decisions are required for the sake of vessel safety. This is a very important subject that requires a firm agreement and commitment between the participants.

Failing to address this issue due to false assumptions is a recipe for disaster. It may be prudent to develop a policy for handling inevitable disagreements when a quick decision must be rendered. By this we mean a mechanism that allows for debate *after* the Captain's decision has been executed.

The decisions we are referring to are of an emergency nature. We recommend that the entire crew be involved in making up the ship's policy while underway, i.e. the use of harnesses, when to reef, watch schedules, etc. One of the advantages of pleasure cruising is that it allows two or more people to participate. Captains should know the fine line that exists between constructive debate that adds to the solution, and petty arguing that adds to the problem.

Even with the most stable couples, emotional outbursts are not optional experiences. They will occur. It is therefore important to have a time-out policy to allow each other some space. There is no way to win emotional arguments while out cruising.

Although there are times when a good heated discussion is required to clear the air, it is also important to know when it is time to give a hug, rather than a lecture.

For the most part, Amy and I are on the same wavelength when it comes to our moods. But there are those times, when lost in the reflection of our individual experiences, that one of us may get down. Sometimes it stems from the boredom of being stuck on a boat during a three-day northerly wind. Other times it is a case of homesickness, wondering if loved ones left behind even remember that we are gone. It is during times like these that respect for each other can turn a bad day into a special one.

One of the best pieces of advice we ever received from some cruising friends was found in the very last sentence of a letter they had sent, from somewhere off the mainland coast of Mexico. We don't remember the advice they gave on weather or sail trim, but we will never forget when they said. "...above and beyond all things you may do, remember to be kind to each other."

The "cruiser's blues" is a real malady that strikes anyone who has cast their lines for distant shores. It impacts even the most experienced folks out sailing the seven seas. It can occur without warning, although we discovered that it seems to hit right after an exceptionally great day. We suspect it is nothing more serious than the post-high let down, like the one we had when Amy got to pet the mantas swimming under our boat and I was able to sell a spare light-wind sail for an unexpected cash windfall, only to spend it the next day correcting problems with our charging system.

As a couple learns to experience incredible natural highs together, they also share the low points. Most long-term cruisers adapt to the lows by allowing them to merely pass of their own accord. Accepting the blues as part of the game can help a couple to practice kindness toward each other.

There is a reward for those who put an effort into preparing themselves along with their vessel. Well adjusted couples find that their relationships grow much stronger while doing their dream. It is a quality that is very apparent when others cross their path.

Yet even in the most adjusted of couples, the inclusion of a third crew member can be all that it takes to unravel their efforts. We cannot begin to tell you the number of folks we have met who experienced major difficulties with crew members they had along on their journey.

A common thread that seemed to run through the worst accounts were the friendships destroyed during the passage part of the adventure. There are some real positives to adding an extra crew member. Watch schedules, emergencies, repairs, and the added conversation, just to name a few.

The downside seems to come when space becomes a problem and tempers flair. On land, friends are able to have disagreements then retreat to individual spaces to assess the argument and purge any hurt feelings. It is not possible to do so in cramped quarters.

It was our experience as a cruising couple that we often assumed our crew member's agenda and expectations were the same as ours. This was not the case.

Often our arguments revolved around considerations of time and destinations. What would have made the trip for us was often in conflict with what our crew member wanted and expected.

These conflicts also tend to involve money. When one is on an extended cruise the impact of money spent is in direct proportion to the amount of time one has left available to continue. And money spent is typically influenced by destination.

Most of the crew members we met were on a vacation. Their expenditures were based on a far more condensed time frame and the consequences of any underestimations were minimal. It was this disparity of agendas that created the majority of conflict. For us to remain in population centers was a surefire way to shave months off our allotted cruising budget, yet for a crew member on board for a limited time frame, the population centers were where the action was. There was no way we could have reconciled this situation.

Although the friendship has dissolved as a result of our conflicts, in hindsight we can now see what should have been obvious right from the start. Three is a crowd on a small sailing vessel, especially when two of the crew are a couple, and one of the couple is captain. It is above the normal human condition to step outside conflicts that affect a couple's relationship and the relationship they have with a third crew member.

After hearing other's stories of problems with additional crew, we have come to realize that no one wins in these situations and the split is often emotional and unpleasant. If we had to rely on additional crew to safely make a passage, we would be sure to make it understood that it is our boat, our rules, and keep the involvement of the other crew member to a specified time frame and destination.

Although we have learned a lot about taking on crew, we have also come to realize that some of the same lessons must be applied when inviting guests to visit from the States. In this area, we have been very fortunate. The guests who have visited were a complete delight and a wonderful addition to our cruising experience. This is a rarity, according to what we have seen and heard from others.

It was common to see how inconsiderate or naive many stateside visitors were toward their cruising hosts. Most land-bound sailors have no idea of the rigors involved in the cruising lifestyle, even worse are those who have never sailed. To these folks, their hosts are on a permanent vacation and they are unable to understand that a week on a cruising vessel has little in common with a catered cruise excursion.

Some of the examples we witnessed were down right funny, like the woman who showed up at a friend's vessel with a hair dryer, cosmetics case, and complete wardrobe, with cocktail dresses and high heels. Some of the not so funny incidents were those that not only affected a cruising couple's relationship, but also friendships they once had with their visitors.

One cruiser we befriended resolved this potential problem by sending her invited guests a detailed explanation of what to expect and more importantly what not to expect. This included how expenses were to be divided among the guests and their hosts.

This may seem unconventional by any stateside decorum, but with the need to keep tensions to a minimum, it is the only way to tip the scales in favor of a fun-filled visit.

How, you may ask, did a sermon on relationships get to be so lengthy? While painting our perspective of the cruising lifestyle with a very wide brush, we viewed all components as directly related to the mechanics of maintaining one's attitude.

The skipper who coerced his reluctant soul mate to go on the dream, the couple that heads out with high expectations and no flexibility, or anyone who has placed a total dependence on their amenities in order to provide their happiness will confront unnecessary difficulties. Every one of these examples will exaggerate the normal difficulties and disappointments freshmen cruisers already face.

We, along with many others, have overcome these disappointments, and at last discovered the beaten path leading to paradise. If you look closely, you may notice a trail of bread crumbs leading off into the distance. These crumbs represent a loaf of wisdom left by those who went before you. Some of the solutions that helped us get through Cruising 101 may also help you during the first 101 days and beyond. ⚓

Chapter 3
The Budget Cruiser

Finding the Means of Escape

> *A journey of a thousand miles*
> *must begin with a single step.*
> —Lao-Tzu

*I*n our cruising adventures, *Free Fall* became a full-fledged character. What started out as a mode of transport evolved into a cherished member of the family.

When a boat becomes the vehicle on the road to your dreams, it takes on a personality of its own. Even the most utilitarian folks we have met could not escape the inevitable bond formed with their vessel. When so much of the cruising experience relates to the home you have chosen, this seems only natural.

The warmth and security of our 30-foot sloop adjusted our attitude during the hard times. The good times we experienced either happened, or were recalled on the vessel we call home. She had become our ambassador of good faith and achievement. Watching your vessel evolve and conform to her intended purpose is as exciting as your first crush. You're not quite sure what you are in for, but you sure like the direction it's going. And it really doesn't matter that she is not a showboat. She is yours, she is willing, and if you have done your homework, she is able. We're talking about the boat now, not the crush.

Exotic destinations remain spectacular whether viewed from a toadstool or a 100-foot yacht. It was our decision to concentrate on an inexpensive, yet safe vessel which would actually allow us to go cruising, rather than merely talk of doing so.

This vehicle of your dreams must be viewed as far more than simply a means of transportation. The attitude you take on board from the beginning sets the stage for your cruising adventure. Placing your expectations on a very basic level—safe transportation and esthetic accommodations—are the fuel for breathing life into what was once an inanimate object.

To utilize your boat as a tool not only to deliver you to distant ports, but also as the provider of a refuge for the psyche is a great premise on which to build.

What you determine as required for the esoteric aspect of selection and/or preparation of your vessel is your decision alone. All we can suggest in the information that follows is the importance of flexibility and the few requirements needed if your level of comfort is kept to the basics.

Disposable Cruising:
Finding the means for a budget escape

If checking out the lifestyle is your primary mission, a "budget cruiser" philosophy provides an almost fail-safe component.

For us it really was a year to count our blessings. We now know that our initial plans to circumnavigate were a real stretch at best, but many of our gut decisions proved to be correct. If given the opportunity to start over, we would still have gone with our '67 Cal-30. *Free Fall* was sound, inexpensive and more than capable of the demands we placed on her. These demands became pretty basic once we permitted ourselves to change many of our goals.

Looking back, we realize many of the compromises we made turned into our best decisions. With a bit of sea time now under our keel, we feel quite confident *Free Fall* will get us through the canal to explore the Caribbean. We are much more at ease with any new chapters we decide to add to our journey, yet we will still feel a wonderful sense of achievement should we ever stop cruising.

The purchase of *Free Fall* for $8,000 was, for us, a perfect solution. Since we have been cruising, that decision has been confirmed by other budget- and no budget-sailors. For those who have not yet purchased a vessel, the "disposable" cruiser may be a viable option.

A disposable vessel is one that is sound (a marine surveyor can determine if she is), safe, simple, and fits the planned time frame for your cruise. It is also an investment you can afford to lose.

If your vessel is to be a floating savings account—something that must be turned back into cash when the trip is over—it does not fit our definition of disposable. When considering the difficulty of insuring a boat in foreign waters, it is simply another burden a blossoming cruiser would fare better without.

The loss of a boat is devastating, even if the survivors escape unharmed. If one's entire life savings is attached to their boat, a loss will be that much more difficult to overcome. The overall cruising experience will have fewer distractions if the fear of losing a large investment is eliminated. If you consider your investment to be the price you are willing to pay for the experience, regardless of the outcome, we are on the same wavelength.

The game becomes all the more enjoyable when a vessel can be purchased and equipped using little money and lots of ingenuity. This also helps motivate you when the molehills begin to look like mountains.

Everyone likes a deal and there are no better deals than knowing you enjoyed over a year of cruising for less than the cost of a family sedan. Hundreds of pre-1972 plastic classics dwell in the harbors of Southern California alone. Cals, Coronados, Islanders, Cheoy Lees and Pearsons, along with many others, have made their appearance in the world's cruising grounds. These are well-constructed fiberglass boats built before the oil crisis, at a time when cost considerations and the liberal use of resins did not go hand in hand.

Walk along the gangway of any marina and you will see these gems sitting weather-worn in their slips. A neglected appearance can indicate the potential to be purchased for a song. We have seen several deals in the six- to eighteen-thousand dollar price range, perfect for trying on the lifestyle.

Although we are not expert sailors or boat builders, we have learned something about what you want to look for when searching for the ideal budget cruiser.

Do not be discouraged by a negative first impression. Often a weathered appearance has little to do with overall condition, unless it is obvious structural damage. If you expect to find a vessel that looks like a million bucks selling for pennies on the dollar, we suggest the ship in the bottle route.

Older vessels detailed to look like new are not where you find bargain basement prices. These boats are on the market with hopes of a top dollar return. The gems tend to be vessels that appear abandoned, ones that became another's money pit.

When you begin your search and inspection of possible candidates, walk down a gangway and look for weathered vessels rather than For-Sale signs. Try to visualize what these boats would look like with a coat of fresh paint and clean and oiled teak work. With a few hours invested on a weekend, you will soon begin to eliminate those boats holding no esthetic interest to you.

Once the field narrows, start leaving notes stating your desire to purchase the vessel. In no time you will be contacted by an owner, or more than likely his or her spouse. Often you will find that the owners of these weathered candidates have made no real attempts to put them on the market.

The more call backs you receive the better the chance for a deal. Having several deals to compare is the perfect place to be. Do not be surprised if an owner is not only open but enthusiastic about selling to some-one who intends to fulfill their former dream. This was the case with the man who had owned our Cal-30.

When we found *Free Fall*, newspapers dating back to the early eighties covered her cabin windows. Large swaths of mustard yellow paint were peeling off her interior. Tons of assorted boating items, along with half-completed projects littered the cabin. Did we mention the avocado shag carpet?

Even in this dire condition, however, we could see her potential. Our seller was gracious (or shrewd) enough to allow us to go down to the boat and sit on her, prior to presenting him with an offer. With cups of coffee in tow, we would come to visit her unsupervised and discuss our future adventure. This went on for several months, until he accepted our offer.

The owner seemed excited about our plans and reduced his price to help us act on them. After talking with other budget cruisers we discovered our deal was not unique.

Although *Free Fall* appeared weathered, she was a relatively unused vessel. After a stem to stern inspection with the advice of some experienced friends, we knew we had found a great disposable cruiser. She fit our criteria for price, condition, and esthetic appeal.

Important things you should look for on possible candidates begins with a preliminary top-side inspection. Check for overall condition of the hull and inspect for stress cracks or any noticeable repairs. Obvious damage should disqualify the vessel, yet there are other indicators to help you determine her condition.

How do the bow and stern railings look? Are they bent or dinged? Are they too shiny for the year of the boat? Don't hesitate to ask for explanations once you have set up an appointment with the owner.

When the two of you do get together, move on deck and inspect the condition of the non-skid. Is it worn smooth? If so, the boat has been used frequently. If not, she has probably been sitting in her slip unused.

Check the mast and boom. How do they look? Are they straight, oxidized, dinged?

Look at the gooseneck and mast track. Anything bent or misshapen?

Be sure to check for cracks in the fiberglass around the compression pad (where the mast sits on the deck) or unusual wear at the base of the mast where it passes through the deck. Are there any large gaps around the shroud and stay anchor points where they pass through the cabin roof?

If things appear to be in order they probably are. Most vessels, especially ones that look unattended, give a fair indication of their condition. If they pass your initial inspection, move below.

There are many indicators you can use to assess a vessel's condition once you have gained entry to her cabin area. Look at the hull liner. Any obvious leaking from the deck to hull joints will be indicated by water stains. Ask for explanations about any water found in the bilge, especially if the water is salty.

Check for any cracks in the fiberglass roving that attach interior bulkheads to the superstructure. It could be an indicator that the boat has seen some hard sailing in its time.

Don't forget to look at the bottom sections of any woodwork. Are they stained? If so, it indicates the vessel took on water. Why?

If any of the owners' explanations leave you with a bad feeling it should not be ignored. There are too many older vessels in excellent shape to choose from.

Doesn't it seem logical to pay a little more for a vessel that shows acceptable wear and tear than to try and get a bargain basement project? The time and expense of major repairs usually negates any deal you thought you had struck.

Keeping that thought in mind, there are other items to check if your candidate passes the initial inspection. Through-hull fittings and subsequent hoses for plumbing should be checked for integrity, along with other obvious items, like fuel hoses, connections, packing glands and rudder and shaft clearances.

The condition of electrical wires or switches must be checked for corrosion, a common problem for vessels that have sat a long time in their slip. Shorts in any DC system pose a real fire hazard on board.

Running and standing rigging should be replaced with oversized wire and halyards, unless this was done recently, and there is no sign of fraying around the fittings.

Sometimes the condition of the auxiliary power plant is the reason you can find a deal on an otherwise sound vessel. Often a motor will deteriorate from non-use. Research the repair or replacement cost of any inboard engine, preferably diesel, along with the other items mentioned.

The price you end up paying should take these costs into consideration. The good news is that most boaters are honest folks. Previous boat owners were always candid, enthusiastic and willing to assist with any questions that might surface even after the deal was transacted.

Not everyone has the patience to spend the year required to find a vessel, prepare it, and tie all loose ends before departure. With some of the new rules at stateside marinas, even those who want to do projects while tied to the slip are not able to. Many marinas do not allow owners to refurbish their vessels on-site, due to both noise and environmental pollution.

For those who want to experience the lifestyle now, there are other options for acquiring your means of escape. Either the trailerable cruiser or an on-site purchase work well, and both have many advantages.

The Trailerable Cruiser

If you are among the folks who do not have enough time for passage making and want to maximize your time in a cost effective manner, consider purchasing a trailerable sailboat.

There are many 25- to 28-foot vessels that have been transported over land and launched in the Sea of Cortez and other cruising areas. This method seems extremely practical for those who do not want to spend their time on outside passages, or could do without the adventures and hazards offered by the Pacific.

One cruiser has done the San Juans, Sea of Cortez, and Caribbean on a 28-foot trailerable sloop. Another family we know had such a great time in their 26-footer they decided to extend their experience. If we didn't already own *Free Fall*, we would give this concept serious thought.

The On-Site Purchase

By purchasing a vessel in the area where you would like to cruise, you can immediately begin your cruise. Those of you who shy away from big projects can find bargains on location, ready to go. As of this writing, many are available for as little as fifty percent of their stateside value. Remember, you are buying another's high expectations gone wrong. Some are in good shape and come fully equipped, while others are picked clean from their inventory and may be far from seaworthy.

The ideal time to search for a sound vessel is right after a boat has arrived from a trip down the outside or just before it heads back up the coast. For Mexico, the prime time is November and late May. If you do so, you may meet a few cruisers willing to turn their vessel over to new owners, rather than turn north up the Pacific, against current, wind, swell, and time.

The truth is, cruising is mostly spent at anchor. Many cruisers readily admit that passage making is not all that it is cracked up to be, especially with long rides to weather. The possibility of locating training wheels in your new backyard is highly probable, if you know what you are getting into.

Numerous fixer-upper boats are available outside the United States for you to work on while vacationing in exotic ports. But beware, unless you are like some folks we know, a two week standard vacation should have your project ready to go cruising by the mid-21st century.

Some of these fixer-uppers need some major fixing up. Many of these vessels have been sitting unattended for years on their anchor, and their effects are apparent. Some have soft spots on their hulls and are taking on water. Quite a few of them are not safe enough to relocate under their own power. The logistics involved with delivering them safely to a boat yard for repairs is complex and risky, and access to supplies limited. But if you back up your purchase with knowledge and patience, great deals can be had.

There are so many inexpensive ways for dreamers to become doers. It amazes us that so relatively few have yet to act on their dreams. After spending our first year in paradise, we know that as long as the vessel is sound it need not cost a fortune to enjoy the cruising lifestyle. In fact, it is unbelievably affordable.

The bottom line is to keep things simple. This applies to purchasing your boat and/or preparing and equipping the one you own. ⚓

Chapter 4
Preparing the
Budget Cruiser

Reaching Escape Velocity

*In things pertaining to enthusiasm, no man is sane
who does not know how to be insane on proper occasions.*
—Henry Ward Beecher

We have come across so many people with ingenious solutions to getting a vessel ready for an
extended cruise, it's a wonder NASA hasn't employed
some of these folks.

Those who have owned their vessel for some time
may have already completed much of the preparation
for getting underway. With that in mind, we decided to
provide the following information and philosophies
for those with the disposable cruiser.

If you feel like we did the day the ether wore off from our purchase of *Free Fall*, you are probably standing in front of your structurally sound but cosmetically disadvantaged investment, wondering what you have gotten yourself into. After the initial cash outlay to purchase your dream, you are looking at more expenditures than your wallet can afford. Don't fret, there is a great and inexpensive place to start, as our own experience will illustrate.

Standing in the main salon, surrounded by at least ten years of accumulated boating widgets and half-empty varnish cans, it became obvious we had a long way to go before ever seeing blue water. And, as if that was not enough enlightenment, we quickly realized it would be hours before we would have a place to sit down.

After throwing away unnecessary items, we cleared a space in our apartment to store sail bags, cushions and the plethora of equipment that would only be in the way on *Free Fall*.

With an empty boat to match our wallet, we did the only project we could afford: scrape and paint the interior. Armed with paint left over from an apartment we had refurbished, we began our first real project. We needed to see an immediate improvement in our investment, if only for the purpose of motivation. The only real value to this bit of information may lie in the boost it offered our morale, one of many jump starts we would need over the course of the next twelve months.

Starting below decks is not a bad idea. Chances are you will find enough projects to keep you busy without spending any money. You will also be spending time in an area where many innovative ideas will be hatched while discussing future adventures.

Only your imagination limits the decisions for adding extra space and useful built-in amenities as long as you rely on common sense.

Visualization is an excellent method for putting your ideas through a conceptual safety test. Any modifications to a cruising vessel in the vein of add-ons or attachments, above or below decks, must be carefully thought through. Before giving yourself a go-ahead, ask yourself a few questions.

How will this modification hold up if the vessel was on her beam ends or even worse, completely upside down?

Will the addition or modification hamper access to vital systems on the vessel such as sea-cocks, engine area and packing gland? Although an unused quarter berth may be a great storage solution made better by enclosing the partition to reduce engine noise, it may also raise the panic quotient if you need to access a stuffing box that begins to act like a busted fire hydrant.

How will weight distribution be affected after completing the modification? Storing books over the batteries next to the auxiliary water tank under the sink on the starboard side, may cause your vessel to list.

Does the modification hamper the structural integrity of the vessel? Even something as stupid as that lip you stub your toe on moving in and out through the forepeak doorway is a structural component.

And last but not least, what would an add-on component do to someone thrown against it in rough weather? Even nicely rounded protruding objects hurt the human body when slammed unexpectedly against them.

Using these questions as qualifiers before starting any new projects will go a long way to adding a sense of security in your new home. Knowing you used your head will affect your attitude positively, especially the first time you experience an adverse change in weather, with no unnecessary bruises.

Not all the preparation on your vessel need be so precise. Interior decorating is one of the more gratifying aspects of preparing your boat for an extended adventure.

Attention to detail below decks is a major consideration for cruising. Liberal use of colored fabric and throw cushions, along with framed personal photos adds much to the warmth of a main salon. And using a light colored paint on some of the wood bulkheads tends to increase the feeling of space.

Although a bit rough on the outside, *Free Fall* has surprised many visitors who have been below in her cabin. The small personal touches have enhanced the quality of our lives on board, providing us with a real sense of home. If you decide to adopt the disposable cruiser philosophy, interior modifications need not be costly to be effective.

Some of our own modifications include a built-in galley and pantry where a rusted alcohol stove and oven once resided. With the help of a friend, we designed and implemented changes using his carpentry skills. We used a propane camping stove and pressure cooker in lieu of a stainless marine unit, saving about $500 in the process.

Other inexpensive enhancements include a built-in Nav station and a fold-down desk for our laptop computer, a modified compartment that holds two 108 amp-hour deep cycle batteries and a host of space modifications for storage.

We derived much of our savings by using epoxy-treated plywood covered with Luan facings. For the time frame we placed on the use of *Free Fall*, we could not justify marine grade woods. So far, knock on wood, nothing below deck shows any signs of a bad choice in materials.

When rewiring our vessel using marine grade wire terminating to a lighted 12-volt fuse panel, we began to see other dramatic savings. We purchased the fuse panel at an electronic hobby shop, along with a volt and amp meter.

Since then, we discovered an excellent solution for monitoring a ship's 12-volt system. A digital electronic multi-tester that plugs into jacks wired in-line with your system will provide you with all the information needed to ascertain your vessel's amp-hour and voltage usage. Total cost for this system runs about $170, saving you $400 over a marine designated system that does little more.

Rounding out the savings below deck was our use of indoor-outdoor carpeting. We spent all of twenty dollars with leftover material to boot. The cabin sole of a cruising vessel takes a lot of abuse, whether covered with carpet or not. Sand, salt water and food always finds its way to the floor, and trying to stay on top of cleaning an expensive carpet is akin to getting stuck in a revolving door. Inexpensive covering with a few cheap area rugs will do the trick when it is time to freshen up the interior.

Although boring when compared to the fun of below deck enhancements, above deck preparations are necessary for the safety of the vessel.

Any area topside that could possibly allow water to end up inside your boat must be addressed. Hatches, ports and companion-way entrances must be modified to ensure they remain fixed and closed to the outside elements.

It is easy to underestimate the force of even a small wave breaking over the decks, and the amount of water it contains. Wave and water management is paramount if heading out for blue water. Vessels have survived full rolls because of the attention an owner put on keeping hatches battened and ports secured during storm conditions.

One of our first major modifications was installing new cabin windows. Using thick tinted Lexon to replace the leaking production units that came on the vessel, we now have great visibility and ports that hold up to big seas. During this project we also added a few opening ports for light and ventilation. These were close-out plastic models we purchased for a bargain. They have held up thus far with no leakage.

Another topside add-on was new oversized rigging, both standing and running. The rigger who installed the new wire was honest enough to point out that the original standing rigging was serviceable, but we decided to go with the new and improved stays and shrouds for our own state of mind.

We mention this to help the reader separate the "fluff" from the necessities. In areas that deal with structural integrity, your piece of mind is a necessary component. Any equipment replaced in that vein is, in our way of thinking, mandatory.

Other added improvements include a stern rack to hold propane and gas jugs and a bowsprit pad with roller system for anchor chores.

We were also interested in our vessels appearance. After getting a $2,200 quote to repaint the top-decks, we bought some Brightside urethane one-step, and completely repainted the decks ourselves using a single quart of paint. The results were amazing and have held up well. Total time to mask and paint: three days.

Almost all the work on *Free Fall* was a mixture of physical labor and plenty of sitting in the cockpit dreaming out loud. The total time without breaks to complete the majority of our projects would have amounted to about three weeks, had we worked around the clock. Looking back, we are glad we spent the extra time.

While preparing *Free Fall*, we found that many folks on the gangway liked the idea of what we were planning. One morning we arrived at our slip to find a used rocker stopper lying in the cockpit, an anonymous gift from one of our silent supporters. We decided that day to keep a mental record of our equipment miracles.

What we have added since that morning, without cost or at a fraction of the market value, was a 33-pound CQR, 100-feet of 5/8ths chain, lifeline webbing (thanks to a couple of volleyball nets), a mizzen sail cover placed over a hanked and sheeted head sail, a thick foam forepeak mattress, cockpit cushions, a sailing sabot to replace our lost Avon and an ancient Horizon VHF radio (still in the box).

The most valuable data we gleaned from our first year out, after shifting our game plan to the disposable cruiser mode, was that we now *know* we want to experience more of the lifestyle. Unfortunately, aspiring cruisers do not have the luxury of experience to qualify their beliefs.

You have to act on your own faith, staying motivated from the day you gave seed to an idea, to the day you give it birth. And preparing your vessel for takeoff can be just as painful, especially to the pocketbook. Setting achievable and affordable projects on a realistic time schedule is necessary for your peace of mind. Make a big deal of crossing off completed projects on your to-do list as soon as these tasks are achieved. If you are to keep your dream alive, you must feed it hope and water it with perspiration.

A realistic itinerary and willingness to adjust your viewpoint often provides the correct decision when preparing your vessel. It even helps when choosing what equipment to bring along. Preparing and equipping a cruising vessel is generally completed simultaneously. Although, to acquire the best deals, those items which cost a lot but take little to install should be purchased just weeks before leaving. Always remember your number one goal is to go cruising. The less time and money spent gathering equipment or chasing after the ever elusive perfect yacht, the more time you have to participate and adjust to your new way of life. If you become grounded in the details, you just may miss the boat. ⚓

*Ground tackle
is the umbilical cord
to life on the hook...*

Chapter 5
Equipping Your Vessel

Zen and the Art of Equipment Failures

> *Our life is frittered away by detail...*
> *Simplify, simplify.*
> —Thoreau

The stage has been set and the players have their scripts in hand, but before the lights are turned on and the action begins, final preparations must be made. How you handle these final details can determine whether your private movie becomes a blockbuster or a bomb.

Both a sound vessel and relationship provide a strong foundation for the success of your cruising plans. It is premature to breathe that sigh of relief, however. Inhale deeply, because it could be some time before you can exhale on the date of your departure.

Now is the time for the flurried action, discussion, confusion, and disillusion for turning your dream into an escape machine. Equipping your vessel before takeoff may seem a simple task, yet many folks have lost their momentum at this point of the commitment, their dreams crashing onto shore.

Corporate America would have you believe that you cannot leave home without their wares. But unless you have limitless funds and a giant yacht, you will not be able to purchase all of them. The process of determining what equipment is necessary is both confusing and frustrating, mainly because this topic is highly debatable based on personal experience.

Dealing with Conflicting Advice

Often after the purchase of our vessel, others would come to advise us on our project, offering their viewpoint as to what a cruising vessel must be. If they had spent any real time cruising, we would pay close attention, but of those we talked to, few had.

It is very easy to be discouraged by others' advice, especially if you are unqualified to refute their alleged expertise. If talking to a qualified marine electronics guy about that subject or to a sailmaker about sail trim, these people are experts who know far more than most about their field of en-

deavor. Does that mean they are experts on cruising? Chances are, unless they have been, they know as much as you do about your dream.

A way to qualify the "can't go without this" crowd is to simply ask if the advised equipment was mandatory on their extended cruise.

When we asked, some egos may have been bruised when the answer was no, but like you, we had a major need for information based on actual experience.

This is not to say we didn't get some useful tips from folks who had yet to head

Each of us has an individual level of comfort which must be met before fun is possible. More importantly, we all have our own considerations for what makes a vessel safe before we jump onto that E-ticket ride.

To dispel much of the confusion, reflect upon the scores of circumnavigations completed with little more than a short sail inventory, jury-rigged self steering, and a sextant for navigation.

Not long ago, a sea bucket to serve as the commode was considered standard fare. Starting from this foundation, there is nowhere to go but toward a more comfortable and safe environment.

To begin putting together a workable program for equipping your vessel, prioritize your spending and

out. Many great ideas are hatched by dreamers visualizing solutions to problems they expect, and it was fun to speculate with them. We were also fortunate to find gangway friends in the midst of preparing their boat for a second time out.

They knew what they needed based on previous experience, but also knew what we could safely do without.

When evaluating advice, it is prudent to question its validity based on actual application and experience. Even then it may only be a qualified opinion that does not pertain to your plans or budget.

What is finally decided on is a decision you must make, especially when trying to determine the category your equipment needs to fit into.

We found much inspiration reading Tania Abie's *Maiden Voyage* and Robin Graham's *Dove*. Books that chronicle real sailing adventures speak of how little one really needs. They also illustrate what cruisers went with, before there were options like the GPS and water-makers.

Elaborating on Micronesian sailors with thatched leaf rafts and pigeons doing the navigation would be overkill, so hopefully you get the point.

equipment needs by category. Although many purchase decisions will be determined by the amount of funding available, there should not be too much debate if we list the categories in this suggested order of priority.

- Safety equipment
- Required support systems
- Comfort amenities

After making your list and determining the priority of each item, hundreds of decisions still need to be made. Confusion will come up and needs to be sorted out. Take just the decisions necessary in the first and most important category to illustrate what we mean.

What constitutes mandatory safety equipment is still a passionately debated topic. Should a self-contained life raft be included? How about a 406 EPIRB? A "ham" radio system?

For us, these items were deemed unnecessary to maintain our feeling of safety. Our decisions were based on acceptable risk and their absence never left us feeling uncomfortable. It is a balancing act, no doubt, as is the entire game of cruising.

Although many grey areas surface when making decisions about equipping for safety, there are those items that should not be ignored, ones that we would not leave home without.

- Man overboard gear
- Fire extinguishers

- Safety harnesses with jack lines
- PFDs, flares, airhorn
- VHF radio and a radar reflector

Ground tackle is the umbilical cord to life on the hook. This is where a great deal of attention and available funds should be paid. From our personal observation, many seem to dangerously skimp on this equipment.

You have a 99 percent chance of dragging anchor at least once while out cruising. Without the proper gear, dragging your hook or experiencing a ground tackle failure can be disastrous. A poorly set anchor poses a greater risk to life and vessel than encountering a storm underway. The enticingly pretty shore can become a menace as fast as the wind turns.

Allocating funds to purchase an oversized main anchor, a subsequent backup, and enough chain and rode for both will go a long way in reinforcing your confidence the first time gale-force winds roar through an anchorage.

Although we will leave the choice and research of anchors up to you, we will offer our suggestions on the use of chain and rode. In the area we cruised and the depths of water where we anchored, we found that 100 feet of chain and 300 feet of nylon braided anchor line worked well. Our backup anchor, also doubling as a stern hook, had the same length of rode with 50 feet of chain.

When not used off the stern—and seldom is there a need to do so—our backup anchor was set for deployment from its stern mount with chain and rode leading forward toward the bow.

Knowing we could toss our stern hook overboard, in the event our primary ground tackle failed provided a tremendous sense of security. All too often we were called upon to assist with the rescue of a dragging vessel. When no backup anchor was there to stop the advancing missile, the situation quickly escalated into a nerve-wracking drama.

Any land surrounding an anchorage has the potential of becoming a lee shore. Getting your boat re-stuck to the bottom is paramount to her survival. If you heed this advice, your boat, and consequently your experience in paradise will be saved.

In recent years, placing a Global Positioning System (GPS) on board has become an important and extremely useful piece of technology. For the cost of this amazing product, we cannot imagine going without one. The margin of error using only manual navigation skills will trivialize the cost of a GPS, especially when tired from pulling watches during a long passage. Due to the recognition of our own capacity for making navigational errors, our Garmin quickly became mandatory safety equipment.

Now that we have learned the power of its menu driven program, we also fit our GPS into the comfort equipment category. Two categories filled by one piece of equipment, now that's saving bucks.

The price of these units continue to drop, while the technology increases. When we got back to the States we were blown away at the low cost of the hiking units. There were several priced under $200. We plan to buy one as an emergency backup to the Garmin 50 we now have on board.

The following items round out our own safety equipment checklist. A good first-aid kit and corresponding medical manuals, short-wave multi-band receiver, spare hand-held VHF radio, foul weather gear, oversized standing and running rigging, a bagged storm sail, plenty of tie-down straps, a warp line for slowing down the speed of a vessel, underwater epoxy with a collision matte, some kind of drogue for heaving to, a length of garden hose to be used for chaffing gear, wet suits in the event of cold water immersion, sailing gloves with added palm protection, sunscreen and sunglasses, headgear, and last but not least, a well thought out policy and procedure for using all safety equipment on board.

Radar is one of many available safety items we have not yet mentioned. Considering the trend of falling prices for previously expensive items, we would have to say that cruisers have many new options to choose from. What is important is the attitude you evoke when adding equipment, especially with limited funds. The real risk of going without radar, for instance, can be reduced by keeping alert watches and avoiding unfamiliar areas when visibility is hampered by fog or lack of daylight.

Safety First is the catch phrase when sorting through your decisions, as is acceptable risk. If you feel your attitude will suffer without certain items and you have the funds or are willing to wait until you do, include any equipment you deem necessary for your own safety.

Support Systems

Moving onto a much lighter topic: required support systems. Much of the equipment that falls into our second category is not that expensive and often not as critical as where you can find them. Extra fuel and water containers are available at major discount stores, along with other clever devices to store food, clothing and even propane for cooking needs.

As you will soon discover, venturing outside the marine industry and using a little ingenuity saves money as well. It will also bolster your attitude when dealing with the myriad of equipment purchases.

There is something very satisfying when you shave 70 percent off the cost of a marine grade item by substituting it with an item stocked at a retail outlet. Always remain cautious when making these decisions. Some products vary little in quality, but a lot in price outside the marine industry. However, other items do not meet marine grade standards and will not hold up to such an environment if exposed to the elements of sun and sea.

Consider all factors before purchasing. Where will the equipment be placed, and how long does it need to last? A lifetime is generally a good place to start, but if your cruise is just for a couple of seasons, why spend the funds if it is not necessary? If a purchase decision has an element of safety attached to it, go with the best marine grade product you can afford.

Using two of our examples may help illustrate some excellent substitutes for our support systems.

Our decision to rely on nonelectric lighting facilitated the purchase of two brass railroad lanterns for the cost of a small gimbaled marine unit. Both lanterns have performed well. They use little kerosene, and offer enough light to read by, not to mention the cosmetic appeal they add to our cabin.

One solution came from the desire to avoid using up our batteries' juice. Purchasing a pump-action 2.5 gallon weed and deck sprayer eliminated the need for electric pumps and we still had pressurized water. Not only did it allow us the luxury of pressurized showers and a way to rinse our dishes, but because it was black it provided hot, solar-heated water.

Many other substitutes will be discovered with a little ingenuity and common sense. A small auto compass found in a discount parts store can be used as a swing indicator in your sleeping area. And while there, don't forget to check out the 12-volt hand-held spot lamps or small dashboard lights that offer an excellent low-draw anchor light when inserted in a salt shaker. If you get by a home improvement center, you may want to pick up a few 9x14 canvas drop cloths. Ours lasted over a year as a sun shade. We simply installed a few grommets and draped it over the boom, with bungee cords to provide tension. Not only did it work well, it was easy to take down in the event of an unannounced blow.

Most of the equipment we talked about in the first two categories may fuel debates, but it should not be such that it adds confusion to your decision. If you found some merit in our basic cruising philosophy and are not afraid to head out on a tight budget, your willingness to be ingenious and flexible will determine many of your next decisions.

You Are Entering The Comfort Zone

Even with the disposable cruiser approach, the most frustrating phase of equipping your vessel is category three: amenities added for comfort. Conflicting information about what is considered comfort, safety or support equipment is a major part of this problem. As you may have already noticed, the best ad campaigns make us feel that a 12-volt marine blender is necessary for safety. Combine that exaggerated illustration with the friends, family and strangers all offering tons of advice, and it is no wonder people who go cruising need time to adjust.

Determining what comfort items to take on board will be a decision based upon your needs, likes, and dislikes. Everyone has a threshold of personal comfort, and if it is not met they will enter the zone of discomfort like a baby minus the pacifier. Some are able to go barebones without it affecting their attitude, while others have high maintenance and no tolerance. Most fall somewhere in the middle, and can make the best of any situation through experience and time.

Since our entire equipment inventory was budget driven, we cannot say with any honesty what we would recommend, for we did not have any comfort amenities other than the GPS, stereo CD player, and laptop computer. We will give a thumbs up to those items.

From the start, as long as *Free Fall* was structurally sound and had our required safety equipment on board, it would successfully provide the platform to determine if the cruising lifestyle suited us.

Countless would-be cruisers remain tied to a slip, waiting to add one last piece of expensive equipment they absolutely must have. The unfortunate by-product to this way of thinking is that once they get that last item, another takes its place.

If your comfort has become dependent upon all the buzzers, bells and technological goodies available, we have some great news.

All over the world's cruising grounds, support groups will help you get through the trauma and disappointment you will suffer as you begin to experience the inevitable break-down of your gadgets, either one at a time or in unison. These support groups are easy to spot. It will be the group on the fringe of a potluck dinner, sharing their technological woes, while the rest of the fleet discusses the whales and the cosmic light show they witnessed the night before.

The point is not how to equip your home, but how to handle those equipment failures mentally. We like to call these moments of tribulation the 'stops.' If the breakdown is serious, it could stop your travels while awaiting a repair. More harmful, however, are the mental stops, which can prevent you from enjoying your paradise. There is an easy solution, simply be prepared both financially and mentally for those inevitable failures.

Most equipment purchased for comfort and convenience perform without any signs of problems when the demands are limited to weekend use and the yearly two-week sailing vacation. Once you head out for an extended cruise, however, the demands will be judged by a whole new criteria. The amount of usage time placed upon your equipment increases a hundred fold over their normal stateside service.

The impact of salt water increases with the miles you put under the keel, as will the need to service the membranes on any water-making devices. Corrosion rears its ugly head on wiring harnesses and radios along with weather-fax equipment. But the dirge of most cruisers we encountered has been refrigeration and charging systems.

Since most of our cruising has been in tropical climates, temperature changes play havoc with the performance specs of add-ons that worked perfectly in the States.

One of the worst mistakes to make while adding additional equipment is to allow yourself to think you are unique and therefore immune to technological failures. We have seen a grown man cry because his bullet-proof systems failed him. Another just picked up his anchor and went home.

If the repair or replacement of your amenities adversely affects your budget, or if you have a hard time accepting the reality that often equipment fails to perform as advertised or expected, we suggest yoga classes before you leave home port. In all seriousness, be prepared to deal with technological woes because they are very much a part of the lifestyle you have chosen. The beauty surrounding you and the wonderful people you meet still exist, regardless of whether your equipment is performing.

Those we have met and admired most are cruisers who list through-hull failures as a time to start worrying. But in all fairness, we have yet to acquire the Buddhist calm of the Through-Hull Faction. The last time we went ballistic was when our marine toilet clogged up. Prior to that it was running out of propane. We must be on the road to enlightenment.

Keep in mind that the less time spent maintaining equipment or chasing after the ever elusive perfect yacht, the more time you have to adjust to a new way of living.

If you decide to equip your vessel with all the bells and whistles, we suggest you shut down those amenities at some point during the first month of your sojourn. See how life is without them. If at the end of your experiment you can turn to your partner and know life is good, go ahead and switch them back on, have a cold beer and know you have become a master of your universe.

We cannot say it enough, the attitude you take on board determines the quality of your cruise, far more than the equipment you think necessary. Once we were forced to create our own conveniences in lieu of missing equipment, we created a list of specific items that might provide some additional luxury. The advantage to making your lists after you arrive in the cruising grounds is the amount of money spent on real versus imagined needs.

One of the equipment decisions we wrestled with prior to leaving was a water-maker. We had been advised that this was considered a safety item. Our cruising budget did not have the funds to get one, so we resigned ourselves to hauling and treating our drinking water. During our time spent cruising, we most often encountered desalinated water, along with mountain spring water on occasion. It was rare to find questionable water which needed to be treated, although it can occur.

After watching a friend of ours spend much of his time going over the performance specs of a water-maker, the episode became the basis for a practical joke. Our friend was involved in a long distance letter tossing battle with a water-maker manufacturer because the product was not performing as promised. A stranger one day announced over the morning net that his water-maker, an identical unit, was performing not only as promised, but better. Naturally the bionic water-maker never existed. The stranger was actually the muffled voice of the local joker living in the harbor. After this incident, we realized we had enough to adjust to without major equipment problems.

Our approach to equipping a vessel is by now obvious. Run what you brung, just don't become dependent on your comfort amenities.

There are so many books written on the subject of equipping your cruising vessel, we figured we would spare you any more details.

What we suggest is that you can equip your attitude if you don't overload it with the same gotta-have-it mentality you left in the States.

The exact same attitudinal approach is our recommendation when preparing your vessel for the big day. We suggest you schedule your equipment purchases for when they are needed. Our reason behind this: attitude control.

For most of us, knowing we just spent $1,800 for a water-maker on the same weekend we had to pay the rigger $2,000 for new shrouds and stays is enough to cause heart palpitations. The net effect is the fear and doubt it may put on your plans. The fact is, you will need to spend some hurt money—paradise is not free. You can reduce your wallet explosions and even trick your brain by spreading out major expenditures. If you need to pick up an expensive piece of equipment one weekend, try to do preparation projects that do not require an additional cash outlay that week.

We bought most of our equipment in their order of necessity on *Free Fall*. After making her comfortably livable with a new paint job, carpeting, and cushions, the first items placed aboard were safety and support equipment. Like many, the list of items we wanted to take was endless. When we neared our date of departure we were nowhere near the end of our wish list and were unable to afford the remaining items. Fortunately, all the equipment *needed* for our journey was already purchased and in place.

When we decide to put a few more miles under our keel, we will go back to the list, but it is normally updated through experience and wisdom. You may want to consider some of these items prior to leaving, but keep in mind, if we had no other option than our current equipment inventory, we would still go. Adaptability to what is, rather than frustration over what we think should be, has been the greatest lesson learned so far. ⚓

*What seemed a necessity
ended up as added
weight, and many spur
of the moment purchases
became priceless.*

Chapter 6
Boat Modifications

Hindsight is Better than No Sight

If a man will begin with certainties, he shall end in doubts,
but if he will be content to begin with doubts,
he shall end in certainties.
—Francis Bacon

Never in our wildest imaginations did we plan to be minimalists. Certainly we hold nothing against the marvels of technology, up to and including that wonderful box which keeps the lettuce from wilting and the beer cold. The point is, if we had more funds available, we would have enjoyed spending it on goodies for *Free Fall*.

For our first time out, going bare bones was incredibly beneficial. We were out there doing it, rather than tied to the sidelines hoping to resuscitate a budget annihilated by equipment costs.

There is little doubt that we gained significantly as humans by discovering life does not end in the absence of hair dryers and blenders, coffee-makers and refrigerators. And a great eye-opener was provided through what was most missed while cruising. Once you determine what you need and what you really want, you have a realistic list of purchases to make. No better environment than that of cruising can determine what equipment works, and what is best left on the shelf at home.

The beauty of making our wish list after we arrived in the cruising grounds is the amount of money we saved. We were able to distinguish between real versus imagined needs by being out there. What may have seemed a necessity ended up as added weight, and many of those spur of the moment purchases turned out to be priceless.

Some of our best solutions were borrowed from vessels anchored alongside us. Not only did we create our own solutions, we also drew from the workable results of others. The wealth of information available through the salty few who already experienced the lifestyle should be utilized.

Since we have returned to feed the kitty we decided to add a few items and modify some of the procedures we use. All of our modifications reduce the cost and effort required by our present systems.

We left port thinking our alternator and Honda generator were sufficient for our charging needs. For the most part this was true. What we did not count on was the hassle of refueling. Nor did we realize that the simple chore of topping off our batteries took up valuable fun time and the noise of our engine and generator became distracting to ourselves and others.

The addition of a solar panel producing between three and five amps per hour was the solution. It is quiet and does not require any effort on our part to produce the energy needed. On our present 12-volt system we run a VHF radio, stereo CD player, and a laptop computer. With solar energy we have the option of using a small inverter to run our printer, charge our power drill and take a small 12-volt vacuum cleaner on board.

Conservation of our batteries is always difficult. They used to require charging every three to four days by either starting the motor or using the generator. With the addition of solar panels, our batteries remain topped off on a daily basis and provide extra power.

By remaining consistent with our effort reduction policy, we found our above deck water jugs required more labor than necessary. We had originally pur-chased them to provide extra storage space below decks. The constant use of our water jugs, along with the sun's intensity, quickly dwindled their numbers. Although our rate of water consumption is down considerably from our first few months of cruising, a trip ashore is still necessary every other day. Water containers are clumsy and heavy, and it is no pleasure to tow them around by cart or dinghy. Water availability varies from port-to-port, and is sometimes inconveniently located and requires quite a walk or ride.

Once again reality proved far more accurate than predeparture speculation. We now realize that we have ample storage below, more than enough to install a 20-gallon water tank. Based on our known consumption, this addition should be sufficient for up to a week.

A chore we underestimated was dropping the hook. Maybe more important was the effort required to raise it. Despite plenty of practice, now and then we did encounter the odd spot where our anchor refused to set. Often we doubted the proficiency of our drop or the quality of the seabed for anchoring. Other times, in a crowded anchorage, we misjudged the scope of our neighbors. When we found ourselves in these situations we had no choice but to pull anchor manually and try again. It was an exercise which could be repeated a half dozen times, a feat far more physically demanding than expected when anchored beyond 30 feet. The addition of an electric windless will prevent possible back injuries and allow us easy pick-up, if there is even the slightest doubt about our holding ground.

Many of the modifications we made prior to departure served their purpose during our time out. As we adapted to our new environment, our needs changed, along with the demands we made on our equipment.

Although our two-burner Primus camping stove conserved energy, it also limited our menu selection. We had plenty of time to perfect our cooking skills with some extremely fresh and exotic ingredients not readily available in the States. As a result, we quickly outgrew our means of cooking. Wonders have been achieved with a pressure cooker and camping stove, but we love fresh-baked goods. We have decided to add a Magic Chef three-burner propane stove and oven.

Those who have a propane oven on board, keep it. In the region where we cruise, propane is inexpensive and readily available. Both alcohol and kerosene are difficult to acquire and expensive.

Along with our other underestimations, the shortage of our patience comes back to haunt us most often. Accommodating wind was rare to find. It was rarer still to find the patience required to handle this di-lemma. A sail-only basis for cruising the world's waters is hard for us to imagine these days, but some purists are still out there doing it.

Unfortunately, motoring often is the reality of cruising. Our Atomic 4 has yet to fail us, although it does consume oil and its reliability could be question-able for long distance cruising. With the availability of diesel fuel and its overall range advantage, we are considering a small diesel. The projected fuel savings over the coming years may even absorb the expenses.

The few remaining items we would like to add or modify are not required for the continuation of our adventure. We consider these items luxuries, things we did not have before due to budgetary restraints, but are now within reach.

We left without refrigeration because of the expense of the unit and support systems required. It was not a source of major distraction, as we made it through a Sea of Cortez summer without refrigeration. But we are now considering a small RV propane refrigerator for use at anchor. We have encountered numerous units, and these seem to be the only trouble-free systems. Since propane is inexpensive and simple, we can also conserve on battery amp-hour requirements.

A cooling system will allow us to go a few days without trips into a village for vegetables, and keep any fish caught for a later meal. We have not yet adapted to eating fresh fish at five in the morning.

The remaining scheduled upgrades are items we can fabricate on our own. The first project on the list is a small hard dodger, constructed over the main hatchway. With our trustworthy Tiller-Master, we look forward to pulling watches in comfort even during adverse weather. Staying warm and dry while underway is mandatory for keeping a good attitude and a sharp eye, as we discovered while heading south. And it does not require an elaborate and expensive spray dodger to accommodate this need.

We figure that even with the new additions, *Free Fall* will still be under the $12K mark, total. If purchased with careful consideration, your disposable cruiser will provide you a vehicle for continued adventures. Your reduced investment will also allow you to move about without the constant worry prevalent on high-dollar yachts.

Even if we replace *Free Fall* at some future date we would still look for a disposable cruiser, no larger than 34 feet. The substantial increase in cost to replace items that perform identical tasks serves as a reminder when our thoughts turn to a larger vessel. A bigger boat can represent bigger problems. For us, we have learned to equate time and money as equal rates of exchange. A $200 savings represents a months worth of cruising, an important part of the equation when considering the vessel and equipment. How bad do we want it? We ask ourselves this question to assist the decision process. It would be wonderful if the same process worked as smoothly when sorting through the mountains of sentimental possessions, deciding what to take and what to leave behind. ⚓

The worst event you may have to deal with, while awaiting a needed part, is hanging out in a beautiful harbor, socializing with some great friends.

Chapter 7
Things to Bring

And a Guide for Things
Best Left at Home

*The goal of all inanimate objects is to resist man
and ultimately defeat him.*
—Russell Baker

With logic and a good eye, we should be able to determine the availability of space and its capacity. When the time comes to load the vessel, however, space rapidly depletes while the stress level goes through the mast. People underestimate their emotional attachment to things left behind, especially as this pile quickly dwarfs the items finding their way on board. This may seem a rather simple detail on the surface, yet there are far more ramifications than one would suspect.

Most of us have spent years accumulating possessions by the time we decide to go cruising. Through both the process of acquiring more mass and striving towards upward mobility, we trade up to larger dwellings.

Moving aboard a vessel that is designed to be your new home is the exact opposite process. It is downward mobility. Imagine attempting to fit the contents of a four bedroom home into a hall closet. Certainly the bulk of your possessions must be left behind.

Sorting through all those years of emotional attachments is the real culprit of wasted time and energy when deciding what to bring. It should seem rather obvious that a favorite grand piano or even an entire wardrobe will not fit in a small sailing vessel. But we assure you someone has seriously considered both items.

Firearm Policies Abroad

One item hotly debated topic revolves around the decision to carry firearms on board. Although we toyed with the idea, we maintained our sanity and did *not* bring a weapon.

Knowing the consequences of being caught with firearms by a foreign government and not once talking to anyone who had personally experienced a situation where one was needed, there simply was no valid argument to bring one along.

If any of the stories we heard from others who had a friend who had a friend were true, anything short of a machine gun was useless anyway. Since we have been out, we have not seen or talked to anyone with first hand experience that would change our thoughts. A flare gun could offer a compromise for any fence-sit-

Deciding what to bring along was one of the most frustrating ordeals we went through. Before we offer our suggestions on what to bring, we will tell you what we should have left at home.

What to Leave Behind:

First on the list was about half of the clothes we brought on board. Other than sweatpants and sweaters for cooler evenings and a nice outfit for going to town, life in the lower latitudes is spent mostly in shorts and T-shirts. Extra clothing takes up a tremendous amount of needed storage space required for more essential provisions.

The overabundance of books, games, and art supplies we thought we would have time to use or read was a major over-estimation. Our general rule of thumb: If you didn't bowl in the States, you probably

ters—at least they are legal to have on board.

Who knows what the ramifications are if you actually used one for self defense, when none was needed, like a fisherman coming alongside to barter. Our own policy is to use hand signals to keep an approaching vessel at a distance, if instinct screams to do so. We do not know what the rest of our policy is, since we have never had an occasion to hold off an un-welcome visitor. The bottom line as we see it is this: Do what you will, but realize that your ability to defend yourself with lethal force is a crapshoot at best. Even if your actions were warranted, you will not find much sympathy and understanding when dealing with a foreign country's legal system after breaking its laws. Instead, stay alert to any local substantiated information that warns of danger, and avoid the area.

won't while cruising. There were so many people to see and things to do, we spent little time playing board games or painting. And although we are both avid readers, the current inventory of books tends to be duplicated throughout the fleet.

Tons of spare materials we thought were needed for repairs should have been left behind. Although some stuff is good to have on board, a spare set of spreaders treads close to overkill. Most cruisers bring aboard too much junk, then part with it cheap, as evidenced by trade items announced each morning on the local cruiser net. It would be easier on your storage areas and waterline if you bring only what is needed for emergencies. Leave most of your replacement inventory at the chandlery. Chances are any items you need are in another boat's inventory.

One of the marvels of doing a shakedown in Mexico is the accessibility of replacement parts in the event of a system failure. The worst event you may have to deal with, while awaiting the shipment of a needed part, is hanging out in a beautiful harbor, socializing with some great folks.

What We Brought:
The key is never to underestimate the items you must take on board. Any safety related items should be obvious. Anything that has to do with ground tackle is high on the priority list. It may seem odd to list this as our first item, but it is the one category of

equipment most in demand on the cruiser's net, especially after a blow.

Shackles, swivels and extra rope should be aboard at the time of departure. A back-up anchor and extra chain is also mandatory. Once again, you will most likely drag the hook at least once while out cruising. If you are ill-equipped for a ground tackle failure, chances of damaging your vessel or even losing it only increase. The odds of having a head sail blow out or a spreader failure pale by comparison.

Common sense goes a long way when planning for spares you choose to take on board. The final decision is up to you. We only suggest you think through the time you plan to be out and replace suspect equipment before you leave.

Items you may want as extras include engine cables, filters, fluids, both an emergency alternator and an injector for the diesel, plugs and points for the gas motor and outboard, and a spare impeller. If you use oil lamps below decks, extra wicks are in order, along with spare electrical wire and connectors.

There are a few excellent check lists available in print. Downwind Marine in San Diego offers a free guide covering all your bases, and *Latitude 38* offers useful suggestions as well. But again, common sense should be the ultimate guide. We found one listing an entire pharmacy to carry on board, only to find the same remedies available in Mexico without a prescription and at a fraction of their stateside cost.

Another inexpensive but useful item we carry is a basting syringe, one of the big plastic ones with the squeeze bulb on top. We use this to fill our kerosene lamps without pouring straight out of the container.

One of the true pleasures of packing for your dream is finding off-the-shelf items, which will provide service and solutions for your cruising needs. Although the chandler will get the lion's share of your budget for the boating items you need, many useful purchases are available from sources outside the retail marine establishments. Do some window shopping at home building supply stores, as well as electronics and RV shops. Keep your eyes open, who knows where you may locate the true pearls, like the stove-top cappuccino maker a friend bought for two dollars at a yard sale.

Be sure to allow extra space for diving and fishing gear, along with your baseball mitt and guitar. These are important items that allow you to interact with your new community.

Man or woman cannot live on bread alone, and if you do not have the means on board to make fish and rice a culinary delight, you will think that bread is your only food source. With all the new-found space on your vessel, we hope you will have fun watching it disappear as you fill it with the most important item placed on board: Food! ⚓

Chapter 8
Provisioning

Food for the Body, Mind and Other Living Things

> He was a very valiant man who
> first adventured on eating oysters.
> —James I

One could easily drown in the amount of details prior to migrating south on an extended cruise. Even after equipping the vessel for passage making, and marking the charts to a future paradise, daunting labor still awaits.

Certainly a wise and cautious captain seriously considers the administration of potential events. They are usually of a somber and necessary nature, such as man overboard drills and rules regarding the handling of storms.

With so much attention focused on perilous possibilities, it is easy to overlook positive future events, especially ones taken for granted in the States.

Many of us remember to pay thanks for the bountiful food on our Thanksgiving plates, but traditionally holidays are the only time any serious attention is put toward food and its preparation.

In the States, we often plan our daily meals right in the grocery store, just hours prior to eating. With modern day conveniences and hectic schedules, many have become fast-food junkies. When the growls in our stomach finally reach a crescendo, we quickly pacify it like a misbehaving child.

It is a small wonder that we put such minuscule attention on food, especially when it is one of the most pleasurable experiences we can enjoy on a daily basis. It is only during rare events where we place more emphasis on our sustenance. Whether receiving that unexpected bonus or, if of Irish decent, an unexpected death, typically a feast is part of the ceremony.

Fortunately in the States, with jobs and budgets, little preparation is needed to celebrate any occasion. One simply goes to the local 24-hour grocery store and waits in line. And if shopping proves less than convenient, one can frequent any of the numerous restaurants available, paying by credit card.

If you have plans for long-term cruising, however, you had better give some consideration to provisioning—for both special occasions and simply filling the void in your belly on a daily basis.

Even if you do not put much consideration into eating while in the States, it would be wise to do so before your cruise begins. Eating often becomes the main event in the day-to-day life of cruising.

Many cruisers group together in port and create their own activities. Wonderful, warm friendships quickly develop, and dinner with friends on a neighboring vessel may replace the television of your past life. In fact, many of the activities we participated in were related to a future meal. Diving for clams beneath the warm blue waters of summer, or hunting fresh snapper with a sling became regular events.

Any bounty recovered usually went toward a luscious stew or appetizer, served at that evening's potluck. Rarely did a day go by where we did not make an attempt to gather food from the sea. One of the wondrous parts of cruising is how involved and self-sufficient one becomes in one's survival.

Obviously, all the seafood you collect needs to be served alongside members of the other food groups. Even the most die-hard fish fans have the urge to break their standard cruising diet with an occasional pasta or bean dish. And no civilized American would celebrate Thanksgiving minus the turkey, pumpkin pie, and trimmings. Try finding those items at your local south of the border tienda.

Certainly a fairly wide, and sometimes exotic choice of fruits and vegetables are available for consumption. They are usually inexpensive when compared to stateside prices, although not cleaned, packaged, or in pristine condition like we are accustomed to.

Rice (basic white) and beans (basic pinto) are cheap and abundant. But if you have a love affair with the entire bean colony, you had better come prepared. The same goes for rice lovers.

Vinegar and oil, stewed tomatoes and canned vegetables, along with peanut butter and jelly are all available. But the jelly will be grape and the vinegar will not be the balsamic variety. Canned goods boast inflated prices and the peanut butter may leave a bad taste in your mouth.

The convenience and variety to which Americans have become spoiled by, and accustomed to, simply cannot be found across the border. A trip to the local tienda can be a difficult, day-long operation. If you limit your travels to the tourist attraction towns, with marinas, taxis, buses, and plenty of shops, your adjustment period should not be too dreadful, although your pocketbook will surely protest. Beware, your year long cruise may shrink to a few months in such environments.

If you want to go off the beaten path and discover those uninhabited islands you have been dreaming about, throw all notions of Americanized service and convenience right out the port window.

Heap your vessel full of products you really need, and those you really love. Following such advice will be rewarded when you sit down to your first sunset feast while anchored off a hidden paradise.

Provisioning and Your Peace of Mind

In our eyes, provisions have become a savings account held within our cupboards. With those items, along with a bit of luck fishing, and a lot of luck sailing, we are nearly self sufficient, without relying on greenbacks for sustenance.

If stocked well, trading flourishes in the cruising environment with both locals and fellow cruisers. Quite often, a local fishermen would love to exchange fresh fillets for a cold beer.

Now we are not suggesting to cut your lines with a handful of change and your good looks. A Port Captain would certainly frown upon you offering a beer or dinner, rather than the pesos owed for processing paperwork. And if somebody takes the time to repair your motor or refrigerator, he or she will likely request the almighty dollar.

Fuel, fresh food, repairs, and services all put dents in your budget. Unexpected costs come up, from health care to equipment failure. The more control you have over your budget, the less these situations will affect your attitude.

Since many cruisers have no positive cash flow after quitting their jobs and selling the farm, the constant outflow of money must be monitored closely and cautiously. The best defense is to stay out of the markets and marinas, remaining anchored off the very islands you came to see. A well-provisioned boat makes this possible.

What's Available and What's Not

Prior to *Free Fall's* great leap south, we spent a frantic week gorging her belly full of supplies to last six months. We spent three days simply looking around and noting prices. Some of the best deals did not come from major outlets, but from local markets with sales on canned corn. After maintaining a list of the best buys, we spent two solid days overloading grocery and dock carts.

Realize that when buying in bulk, you wield a certain power over costs. Most stores reduce prices given the possibility of unloading full cases of stewed tomatoes.

When we rung the final tab, over $500 was spent on food, health and hair care products—the best investment we made for the entire voyage.

Mistakes were made, however. Eighteen months later, certain items still take up valuable space aboard *Free Fall*. We got a great deal on a few dozen pounds of split peas. After hours of soaking and cooking those rascally peas, the soup still came out crunchy. Great for cleaning teeth, disgusting for the pallet.

We spent a good chunk of our initial provisioning budget on tinned meats. Vienna sausage, chicken, and turkey. Some were quick-meal favorites of ours in the States, others were great deals in bulk. This decision, too, became a poor one. Once our bodies adjusted to the natural purification of fresh food and fresh air, the well preserved meat tasted foreign and dissatisfying. We are by no means health nuts, but we find the cruising lifestyle naturally healthy.

A medical arsenal found its way on *Free Fall*, with hopes that it would remain unused, and we have been rather fortunate so far. Looking back, however, only the basic needs would have sufficed. From what we have observed and experienced, health problems are handled readily and inexpensively down south with ease. A prescription is not required for most drugs, from antibiotics to pain suppressants, and these over-the-counter medications will serve most needs at a fraction of stateside costs.

Perhaps those funds you have reserved for medications would be better spent on emergency medical treatment manuals. Unfortunately, no warnings are given for accidents, and every member aboard your vessel should have basic first-aid procedures well rehearsed.

The greatest challenge of cruising may lie in the momentous responsibilities woven into the fabric of living at sea. From bringing a crewman back to safety from an overboard spill, to handling a deep puncture wound caused by an unclean fish hook, you must always be prepared to deal with the unexpected.

The unexpected may also entail the sorting out of current and outright false information. When gathering data on what provisions to bring, from medications and guidebooks to foodstuffs, always search for the most current advice. We received a lot of good advice from cruisers who had recently been at sea, and some bad advice from those who had been out a few years ago.The deals of yesterday may be closed today.

Change is constant when considering provisioning. One small change occurred while we were out cruising, and was not observed until we made a trip back to the States for provisions.

Coffee is always a well stocked item on *Free Fall*. It is our beverage of choice. When we originally provisioned, we purchased a great deal of coffee for an exceptional price. However, less than a year later, the price of coffee shot up the mast.

Adaptation being the key to our cruising experience, *Free Fall's* cupboards now overflow with Mexican beans. After experiencing the quality and pleasing flavor of their coffee, it will no longer be on our list of replenishments from the States. Be sure to sample many of the beans available, there is absolutely a difference. Some are sugar coated, and although substantially lower in price, the flavor corresponds as well.

Other items are available just across the border, much cheaper than comparable items in the States. Cereal, in most of the sugar-coated and healthy varieties. Soy sauce, ketchup, mayonnaise, and even teriyaki are not difficult items to locate, especially at state run stores found in most towns. Powdered and boxed milks, soup crackers in individual packets, and cookies, (as long as you are not a connoisseur and prefer crunchy to chewy). Powdered detergents can also be found, along with name brand fabric softeners which help in the removal of salt from clothing.

We will take a chance and be politically incorrect by announcing to all cigarette smokers that basic brands sell at bargain prices. If the lack of a filter does not bother you, a carton of smokes goes for under five bucks. Montanas, suspiciously similar to Marlboros, sell for just over a buck a pack, and even menthols are available.

While on the topic of not so healthy habits, it is also dangerously cheap to drink alcoholic beverages down south. Wine, your basic red and white, along with wine coolers, rum, vodka, tequila, gin, and kahlua, are all accessible. Do shop around, however. Prices and products vary throughout the stores in each town. Your best bet for the lowest prices usually starts at the local state store. But for those who prefer to burn their bellies with a more potent American beverage, like that Mr. Daniel's drink, you may want to stock up before shipping out.

Many items are either difficult to find, limited in variety, or exorbitant in price once you cross the border. Spaghetti and macaroni can usually be found, but if you are a pasta fan, you can get a better variety at a better price in the States. Stock up on salad dressings, or better yet, collect lots of recipes and ingredients to make your own.

Bring along a wide assortment of cheese, but only if you have the space and systems to store them. Some Jack and American can be located, along with a few others, but Provolone, Swiss, fresh Parmesan, and Cheddar are difficult to find.

If you love to have fresh bread to stack your cheese on, developing a skill in baking is a smart move. The bread found across the border has its share of cruiser fans, when fortunate enough to come across fresh baked goods. Eat those treats quickly and enjoy. The pleasure certainly won't last, and those delicacies have the ability to turn into deadly missiles if launched the next day. And if you prefer anything other than white and somewhat sweet bread, you would be ahead of the game by bringing your own ingredients. Fresh bread can't be beat when spending serious time floating in gorgeous anchorages.

Cleaning products are mostly obtainable at very good rates. However, if you have lots of shiny wood down below in your beloved abode, and delight in lemony scents, bring those cleansers with you. Paper products tend to be more expensive and of a lesser quality. Make some room for these bulky products, and use sparingly.

A few other odd end items you may want to stock up on include specialty hair and skin care products, a box of varied greeting cards for both expected and surprise occasions, bulk specialty teas, sunglasses, and stamps.

Nobody will ever be capable of putting together the ultimate list of items needed for an extended cruise. People's needs are much too individual, and the world changes too rapidly, as does the supply. Just remember the Rolling Stones' great wisdom while on your cruise: You can't always get what you want, but you'll always get what you need.

Storing Your Provisions

Purchasing all the items you need prior to your cruise is the easy part. Storing all those items is a hair-pulling and time consuming event.

There are a few quick guidelines to follow before even making the attempt.

No other boat projects can be combined with storing your provisions. All available space will be necessary, both above and below decks.

Unfortunately, storage of provisions cannot be a joint effort. Whoever is the primary cook on board must take this tedious job as his or her responsibility. The cook must know where everything is located.

Some items will be utilized more than others, and their location must be readily accessible.

A detailed inventory list should be made, along with each item's location. By maintaining this list, everything will be available when needed, while exercising more control over wasteful purchases.

We actually created a blueprint of *Free Fall* for this purpose. Each cupboard was lettered. All canned vegetables and fruits were stored in Hatch A. Dried goods, such as beans and oatmeal, were placed in Hatch B. A list containing all items stored in each cupboard corresponded to our blueprint, along with a precise count of each item. Obviously, we had a surplus of some items, such as stewed tomatoes. Some of these cans had to be within an arm's grasp due to their constant use in numerous recipes. An entire hatch could easily be filled with a single item. Excess items should be stored in those hidden and hard to reach cubbyholes, to make the most use of the limited storage space on most boats.

Do not skimp on the quality of storage containers. Make sure you purchase airtight and sturdy plastic containers. Little creatures drill holes into cheaper ones, contaminating your food. Also, make sure you identify every item stored in each container. Flour and pancake mixes, along with several others, look very similar in both color and texture.

On canned items it is a wise idea to identify the contents with a marker on the top of each can, along with the date. Paper labels in moist climates tend to fall off, and your recipes may then become more creative than your pallet.

When provisioning, remember to remove all cardboard and paper bag items before boarding, no matter where you are located. Cockroaches love these environments. Cases of fresh fruit, vegetables, and beer are common culprits.

Limit the amount of glass containers on board. A certain amount of glass is unavoidable, so be cautious when storing and using those items.

The myriad of details surrounding provisioning calls for both a healthy dose of patience and stamina. Fortunately, the time and energy spent now in preparation will be rewarded in the months ahead.

An incredible feeling of confidence and security comes with knowing you have all the ingredients needed for survival on a well-stocked vessel. Your monthly spending can now be controlled or even ceased altogether, without the consequences found in stateside living. In fact, spending a month on an uninhabited island without spending a dime can hardly be deemed as a dire circumstance.

Indeed, provisioning provides more than a savings, but a certain amount of confidence while cruising. When equipment unexpectedly fails, recovering from the expense and getting back on budget is less stressful when no additional expenses are necessary. One may not be able to avoid the uncontrollables, but with some of those proverbial safety nets, provisioning included, the consequences can be limited. But most importantly, your attitude will survive, along with your cruise. ⚓

Chapter 9
The Cruising Budget

How Much is This
in Dollars, Por Favor?

> *I finally know what distinguishes man
> from the other beasts: financial worries.*
> —Jules Renard

The amount of money in one's budget has little to do with how much fun one can extract from cruising. It is a fun-filled lifestyle, for the large part, and most of the pleasurable activities encircling it are free.

Before leaving, however, one of the greatest concerns in the preparation of an extended cruise is determining how much money is necessary to cover all the elements of cruising. A financial safety net is necessary to cover equipment failures, along with any medical emergencies, and these savings should be guarded like a squirrel to nuts. Undoubtedly though, the hardest price tag to determine is that of the monthly budget.

For us, no greater thirst for information existed than the topic of cost. We had read books about growing our own food on board and articles on budgets under $200 a month. Other information advised us to count on a minimum $1,000 a month budget. With such disparity, we determined we were fairly average folks with average needs and took a safe middle ground. Before departing, we set our budget at $450 a month.

Like a bus in the night, an unforeseen financial loss hit us just days after arriving in San Diego aboard *Free Fall*. Our accountant became the bearer of bad news. It was owed taxes with us, but who knows what it could be with you? An unexpected illness? A faulty motor? Even the most precise of plans will unexpectedly meet with some sort of adversity.

We were left with a budget that was only good until it ran out. Only $2,200 was left, after tucking away $1000 for an emergency or our return, whichever came first. All the speculation and careful planning was reduced to taking the plunge to see just how deep the water really was. Unquestionably, it was an appalling, gut-wrenching way to embark on a lifelong dream. With only a commitment and a thousand wishes to the heavens above, we pointed *Free Fall's* bow south. It was our only option. Too much time, energy, and emotion was invested for us to scrap the entire goal or even postpone it for another year.

A do-or-die mentality crept on board and helped provide some lessons. Our original goals were in the two- to three-year time frame. After taking our bad medicine in San Diego, we prayed for a six month trip and headed for Mexico.

It was 15 months later before we made our return, and if ever there was a question in our minds as to the existence of miracles, it has been answered. Our average monthly expenses averaged less than $200 a month, including living expenses, fuel, and basic equipment purchases. Within this budget is the coverage of a few expensive mistakes made on the way down the coast. So some weeks we did not spend a dime.

Not only were we able to extend the cruise for almost a year with our budget, we also learned the power of flexibility when setting out to attain goals. By accepting cruising's uncontrollables and working hard to shift our point of view in a positive direction, we were able to take control of both our cruise and our budget. Once we realized how little was needed to go cruising and still have a blast, the fears we had carried fell like a sack of rocks. We now look at a monthly budget of $450 as wealth.

Within a kingdom of penny-pinchers, we would surely be considered a lavish, jet-set couple. Many folks have made us look wasteful compared with their frugal spending habits. One cruiser left San

Diego with $500 in his pocket. In Mexico a few months later, he still had $300.

Once you become accustomed to the lifestyle, monthly expenses tend to decrease. You will begin to realize that most expenditures are made by decision, not necessity.

Even more important than the amount budgeted for cruising is the policy used for spending. The most effective method we use is to treat money not spent as money earned. Using this philosophy, we save $20 every time we gather clams to eat on the half-shell or snare a snapper's fillet at the end of our fishing line.

The same can be said for repairing an item, rather than replacing it. When money no longer is the sole controller of one's security, there is less fear and fewer heart attacks when your budget needs a serious alignment.

A positive attitude and some improvisation allows continuation of the cruising game. We know one family who said they were so broke they could not pay attention, but their dog was eating lobster. At least in Mexico, with your home packed full of provisions and a fishing pole, there is not much to fear.

Whatever amount of money you decide to take cruising should be based on your needs, and especially those of your boat. But it is much easier on both your attitude and your pocketbook to plan for a shorter time frame to find out how much it really costs.

Hindsight provides great lessons. It taught us that we spent more during our first three months of cruising, while attempting to adapt to a new environment. We also did not take into account future months where we would be able to apply our newfound skills.

When planning for your budget and peace of mind, multiply your monthly budget by three for the first three months of cruising. Newcomers to cruising make mistakes and sustain damages. The loss of our dinghy and outboard was our first mistake, and their replacement knocked a dent in our budget.

If on a shoestring budget like ours, watch where you step. From grocery stores, bars, and restaurants, to the very ports hailed, let the calculator be your guide. The expensive ports enticed us to enter, and we often overstayed our budget's welcome. Food is often more expensive, and there are too many temptations to resist. Fees on slips are expensive, sometimes more so than in the States, and their accessibility and accommodations are tempting as well. We paid $26 a night at one location. Anchoring is usually free.

Settling into a spending pattern does take time. And as part of your attitude maintenance program, learning when to spend is also important.

If a piece of equipment breaks down, and costs $300 to fix or replace, it would be wise to adapt and go without it. If that is not possible, do not be afraid to postpone its repair if not needed while at anchor. Doing this allows you to spread a $300 expense over a few weeks, rather than taking a big hit against a $500 monthly allotment.

When a budget becomes severely tapped, attitudes often take a sharp turn in a negative direction, transforming into a domino waiting to fall. Financial trouble and the stress involved is often the culprit of a heated argument, simply because your stateside experience says you are running out of money and time. Other than unforeseen expenditures, most of how and when you spend money is strictly a choice you control.

We tried at first to keep a written log for every penny spent. This proved demoralizing. We focused on spending after the fact, leaving us feeling we could not afford to do anything. The system we now use is the most simple and effective way to manage our spending while preserving a positive attitude.

If you plan to cruise a foreign country, it is a good idea to convert your monthly dollar outlay into the "coin of the realm." The advantage for this is twofold. First, you are dealing in the same currency that the products are priced. Second, you have the ability to replenish your cash supply in small amounts. This allows you to take advantage of the fluctuating exchange rates and removes any confusion converting dollars into pesos. If you are working in pesos, you should feel richer right from the start.

The method we found incredibly effective is to take our monthly allocation and divide it into a weekly budget amount. We then mark four separate envelopes, from week one to four. These constitute our monthly budget. In addition to these four envelopes we added a fifth, and labeled it savings. (For the remainder of our illustration we will be talking in pesos. At the time this is being written the exchange rate is as high as seven pesos to one US dollar.)

Having marked our weekly envelopes, we put 350 pesos in each and placed week one in a file box with easy access. Our 350 pesos represents a daily budget of 50 pesos.

The beauty of this system is its simplicity. Rather than tracking every expense, we agree to spend only 50 pesos a day. The secret to our success is in the savings envelope. We place any unused pesos in this envelope at the end of the day. We were amazed at how quickly our savings envelope swelled.

Our system tricked us into working only with money on hand, spending accordingly. The fun began when we occasionally tapped into our savings, taking no more than half the total amount.

Suddenly, we felt like we had income as opposed to outlay. When confined to the boat due to "northerlies" or sequestered out at one of the many islands, we were unable to spend, therefore all our daily funds went into the savings envelope.

We now have our budget controlled to the point where we can afford to go out for dinner occasionally. That our expenses have been cut is the amazing aspect of this program. We are now aware of the fixed amount we can spend, instead of just recording how it was spent. We took control of our money, rather than letting our money control us.

From the start, the key to making this system work is discipline. Credit is not available on this program and we cannot borrow from future weeks. If we run out of funds mid-week, we wait for payday.

Adapting to this system is easier than expected. We do not even think about it anymore. We still make a big deal of paying ourselves with a new weekly envelope, along with counting the savings envelope every Sunday morning.

We use the half we left in savings for any large purchases, and so far our savings balance has always been a few hundred pesos. We cannot speak for you, but for us, and the majority of cruisers on a fixed savings, feeling short on funds can be devastating. It places a barrier on everything and has an impact on the perception of time. While cruising, there is nothing worse than having your focus fixed on a deadline, especially when it is attached to fear over finances. It controls every decision you make, out of concern that your trip may be cut short.

In an area like the Sea of Cortez, very little needs to be spent. There is an abundant and inexpensive supply of fresh vegetables, tortillas and rice, along with a wide variety of seafood available. And because so many activities are free, going to town for entertainment is purely a choice out of luxury. We have all been conditioned to believe that everything has a price, even to enjoy ourselves. Not so in Mexico.

It takes time for many to break old habits. Some never do. Some cruisers have incredibly high budgets, and still feel financially restricted. There was one couple reputed to be on a $4,000 monthly budget, and they did not own a mega-yacht with a hired crew. This situation is hard for us to imagine, but it also illustrates the diversity of philosophies and comfort zones in the cruising lifestyle. This aspect of individuality throws many for a loop as they begin to sort through the assortment of people encountered.

The only common thread that seems to run through a cruising fleet is that they have all gone cruising. The inherent challenge is to discover common areas of interest, often times with those you would least expect. We have all been brainwashed to believe that financial prestige and status creates a pecking order. This is not absent among cruisers, the difference is it exists on both extremes of the cruising kitty. It is easy for those living off the land (or sea) to believe their experience is more pure than those on a sizable pension or investment savings plan. We do not subscribe to either philosophy.

One of our most pleasant discoveries while cruising was the explosion of this myth. Good people are good people, regardless of their financial situation. ⚓

*Even cruising veterans
called it a magic year...
We can't think of a more
emotional time than the end
of that summer as friends
began to change course
and seek a new horizon.*

Chapter 10
About the People

It Takes All Kinds to Stock a Planet

Let us be united by everything that divides us!
—Karel Capek

*I*f Cruising 101 were actually a treasure map, this chapter would be the one stamped with an **X**. Incredible riches can be found while cruising, especially after you have learned to jump the quicksand and skip the mires. Incredible beauty and all sorts of adventures are there to encounter during your sojourn, and numerous lessons and skills to be learned. The most precious treasures of cruising, however, are the people you will meet and the friends you will make.

The environment surrounding the cruising lifestyle is an incredibly fertile ground for friendships. With the nine-to-five syndrome out of the way, time to spend with your community is no longer an issue. Open invitation activities from potlucks to anchorage outings are constant, and these social gatherings are great opportunities to meet neighbors.

Then there is the element of need for others in what could become a dangerous setting. Cruisers are self sufficient by nature. They have to be when living without the safeguards available in the States. However, when a crisis presents itself, your only hope for survival may come from neighboring cruisers. Unfortunately, we have witnessed numerous situations of peril, from both sides of the equation.

Just months before we returned to the States, one such crisis hit our little harbor of Puerto Escondido early in the morning. A woman had a strong allergic reaction to some medication she had taken. Her breathing became labored, and her frantic husband called for help over the VHF. The harbor had only minutes to act, and although an ambulance was on its way, the ride was over a rough and dangerous road. The cruisers organized and enacted a rescue. The vessel was moved and side-tied to a dock for easy access to the medical unit. A quick-acting and prudent cruiser gave her a shot of epinephrine. It was this shot which saved her life.

We have witnessed rescue missions during our stay in Mexico, and have participated in many. The most common crisis is that of a vessel dragging anchor, and it usually happens in adverse weather, with a strong blow ripping through the harbor. The dragging vessel becomes a danger to itself and the rest of the fleet, threatening to pull the anchors of other vessels or even T-boning those in its path. Unfortunately, a strong wind quickly discovers poorly set anchors within minutes of each other, and it is not uncommon to have multiple rescues occurring at once. Often times the dragging vessel is unmanned and locked. To stop a boat's movement in such a circumstance takes the strength and speed of many.

Most cruisers make a habit of monitoring their VHFs when aboard, and for good reason. Maydays are more common than expected. You could be in the vicinity of the distressed vessel and be its only source of hope. Many Maydays come from vessels about to be beached by a furious blow or man overboards, but we have heard more than one call where a cruiser's ship springs a leak while out at sea.

The local Port Captains monitor the net, and become involved in rescues. Even the Mexican Navy has saved its share of American vessels in the Sea of Cortez. Most often, however, cruisers band together to save one of their own. The fastest ship, often a power boat, is sent with any needed equipment, along with volunteers most capable of assistance.

The entire harbor often joins in the efforts, offering fuel, supplies, tools or knowledge.

When joining together in such missions, the bonds of friendship and trust are inescapable. Those saved never forget who risked life and limb to assist them in their time of need. We know, after having our own beloved vessel saved in Cabo San Lucas by the *Gosling* and crew. Often those who come to the rescue have been saved themselves at some point in time.

Out of all the fascinating, courageous, vibrant, and loving people you will meet while cruising, many of them develop into relationships beyond that of a buddy. Our extended family has swelled while cruising, and to this day we welcome them into our hearts and our home.

Not all will become your blood brothers, however. Despite all that cruisers have in common, it remains an incredibly diverse group. Each has his or her own reason for cruising. Some people move toward something, while others leave something behind. A few are on an extended but temporary vacation, and to others, cruising is their way of life.

Different styles of cruising have even developed. In the time that we have been out, we have discovered three general cruising factions and each contain a certain amount of insight concerning one's likes and dislikes, needs and fears.

Some folks naturally drift toward the population centers and marinas, with the higher level of conveniences and activities, along with expenses. Perhaps the party pulse calls them to the harbor, or possibly the comforts of running water, a constant flow of electricity and safety from a strong blow.

With others, the wanderlust bug pumps through their veins, or they are living on borrowed time and consumed with a passion to see every anchorage Baja has to offer. They buzz from one spot to the next like a bee sampling the nectar of every flower.

Then there are the shopkeepers. Those who have bumped into a spot so idyllic they have to kick their feet up on the bulkhead and stay awhile. These locations generally offer some sort of natural protection from the elements and have so much to offer in the way of beauty and natural resources, a community of cruisers has developed around them.

Puerto Escondido converted us into shopkeepers, giving us both the key and the insight into the cruising community.

The rugged mountains surrounding the harbor offer protection from strong winds, making it a haven for vessels when hurricanes head up the sea. The conveniences of fresh water and the neighboring town of Loreto, along with the islands beckoning just miles away, have tempted numerous vessels to prolong their stay. It was in this special harbor where we found some answers and made some conclusions about our new and different lifestyle.

About The People

The cruising folks we have met can be described in two words, diverse and capable.

Lesson one for freshmen cruisers: throw away the book of preconceived notions. Most of the visible classifications you used as a measuring stick back home have little or no relevance while cruising.

For many, this has been a source of confusion while struggling to adapt to the lifestyle. Trying to evaluate the type of people you meet based on surface clues will leave you feeling guilty more often than not about how you base your value judgments.

Money and boat size has nothing to do with values or personality. It does not aid or abet the ability to accurately assess a fellow cruiser. But more importantly, your new community will not be using these benchmarks to determine if *you* fit into the group. Personal wealth, or its absence, should not hold you back from finding a common ground with others.

It took us awhile to just sit back and meet other people without forming an instant opinion. Too often the eccentric guy with a pony tail and beads turned out to be an acclaimed professional in his field back home (heart surgery or quantum physics come to mind).

One informative and inspiring couple pursued their dream after the tragic death of their two children. This couple was so enthusiastic and helpful, we were completely unaware of the loss they were confronting and overcoming.

Or how about the flower-power woman we met, whose mouth would put a merchant sailor to shame in both English and Spanish? It did not invalidate the numerous university degrees she held, nor did it discount the valuable friendship we formed, once we got to know her and her husband.

The point is, if there was ever any truth to the saying, *you can't judge a book by its cover*, it was probably discovered while cruising. The sooner one can shed the need for people to look a certain way, or believe in a similar philosophy, the quicker the adjustment to the game of cruising. Often one will begin to gauge the speed of their transition when they realize diversity lends much to the overall scheme.

The logical approach a novice cruiser should take when assessing all the folks in a harbor would be to realize that everyone has already accomplished what they themselves have set out to do. By using this approach, a natural respect may displace an otherwise hasty evaluation.

Taking this approach just one step further, first time cruisers would realize that anchored in front of them are the answers to most questions they may have. Where is the water? Why is my engine overheating? Where do I check in?

When we formed the policy that all folks were worthy of our immediate respect, regardless of their appearance or beliefs, we began to meet what will always be in our minds the most special people on earth. Is that to say there are no real jerks in the cruising game? Absolutely not. People are people, with their good and bad qualities, wherever you may go. But rude, self-serving folks are in the minority and are often turned away from the lifestyle, simply because they are unable to adapt to a harmonious environment.

This life is still life, yet we discovered a valuable piece of wisdom. Just because you do not get along with someone, or rather, have little in common with them, does not qualify them as a real jerk. In fact, if they were in peril, we would assist them in a heartbeat. And they would do the same for us.

To some, good people in a majority may sound a bit too hyped for reality. Yet we found this to be the norm, even though it took us some time to adapt to the "cruising code of good manners."

We cannot help you find ethics, but hopefully we can give you some pointers on etiquette, ones that will help you adjust to the lifestyle and allow those already out a more expedient way of adjusting to you.

Shoes and Shirts Are Not Required

The community of cruisers we have met seemed a bit reserved in our first few encounters. Not that they were rude to us, just that there was no welcoming committee the day we pulled into the harbor. This seems like more of a natural process for group survival, rather than a selection committee. This process is more of a weeding out ordeal than an "exclusive club" mentality.

Most cruisers who have some time under their keel want harmony among their neighbors, and would rather let the relationship form naturally instead of rushing in to form friendships. The diversity that exists among cruisers necessitates this process. It is often better to wait and see how the new guy interacts on the whole, rather than form any quick assessments. We suspect that the absence of a welcome wagon is based on the rationale that the real jerks will show their true colors if left in their own pastures for awhile.

All that being said, we hope some of these tips help you integrate yourself into the community more rapidly. As is common with functioning social groups, rules of the road and acceptable behavior remain cornerstones to a harmonious environment.

The summer of '94 in our hidden port was a testimonial about how well folks interact. Even long term cruising veterans called it a magic year. The season was exceptional and many of the folks we met were captivated by the community that was in place. We cannot think of a more emotional time than the end of that summer as friends began to change course and seek a new horizon. Some went home for the winter, others headed north or south. There were some who came back to capture more of the magic. One family left and came back so often, we no longer believed they were really leaving until we received word from them on their way to mainland Mexico.

In hindsight, a footprint was left, reflecting some evidence as to why the community worked so well. ⚓

Chapter 11
The Cruising Etiquette

Surefire Ways to Get
Invited to the Dance

Civility costs nothing and buys everything.
—Lady Mary Wortley Montagu

Either you can stand outside the harbor with your nose pressed against the window or you can knock upon the door and walk right in. Initially, we found ourselves feeling left out of the cruising community. Once we began to understand the new culture we had joined, watching others having fun evolved into full-on participation.

Stepping off the sidelines and onto the playing field is the best way to become a member of the community. Being the first to lend a helping hand will make you its ambassador.

Money is not the helping hand expected by cruisers or the fleet, unless it is a donation to improve the equipment everyone uses and benefits from. Acts such as the purchase of a new hose needed by the communal water source would be recognized and appreciated throughout the harbor.

If a cruiser is rowing a dinghy full of water jugs, offer a tow. Whenever you see anyone having some sort of difficulty, whether tying up to the water dock or getting their anchor to hold, offer some aid. At the very least, consider these acts as crisis preventive measures. At your best, greet people with kindness and a helping hand. The same considerations will likely be extended to you.

Volunteering for, or organizing group activities, especially those benefiting the community, will help make you an active member. Coordinating a harbor clean-up or gathering enough players for a game of water basketball brings the community out of the doldrums and places them right off your stern, into the realm of friendship.

Offering assistance on the VHF net is another effective way to establish your desire to be a part of the community. Most ports should have active morning nets, usually starting at eight o'clock. And most nets have a local assistance category. From offering rides to town or providing requested information, there is no better format for informing people of your helpful intentions. It is also a great way to begin to meet the people you have assisted.

No one we have met expects a handout, so do not be confused if the people you helped ask if they can pay or barter something for your help. The general rule of thumb is this: if it cost you money, then it is normal to be reimbursed for your cost. If applying your trade is not necessary as part of your cruising budget, offer it in the spirit of the help it may provide. A physical therapist helped one cruiser get back on his feet after injuring his back. Another cruiser offered free introductory courses in Spanish to the fleet. These acts of contribution not only help the community, they also add to one's cruising experience.

The majority of cruisers are more than fair, even those who trade their services or an inventory of equipment they brought along.

Placing a price tag on any help you offer or pricing your services or inventory at a level the market cannot bear is a quick way to be classified as a jerk. Those who continue in this vein often find themselves isolated and without the support of the community at large.

There are other social *faux pas* that will alienate you from the community, if they become an ongoing pattern of behavior.

- Not offering assistance, but always requesting it.
- Locking your dinghy painter on top of the painters that were tied up before you.
- Not offering to replace the contents of an item borrowed, even if it was only a small amount, i.e. oil, gas, diesel, epoxy, sugar, coffee, etc.
- Stepping on a VHF frequency already in use.
- Spreading defamatory gossip.
- Expounding prejudicial viewpoints during a cruiser gathering.
- Becoming loud and obnoxious while drinking.
- "Hitting" on another cruiser's companion.
- Keeping items that are found, without making an effort to determine who may have lost them. Finders-Keepers has no place in pardise.
- Anchoring too close to another vessel, or using too much scope in close quarters
- Leaving your vessel unattended during the first blow in a new anchorage (dragging tends to occur at 20-25 knots and up, especially for those who anchored under calm conditions.)
- Boarding another's vessel, without being asked or given permission to do so, except in the case of an emergency (dragging is a prime example).
- Not offering to help pay for gas if a cruiser gives you a ride to town.
- Running generators in the early mornings, or late in the evenings. Remember, it is not just your paradise.
- Tying up the local water supply to fill up large tank capacities without informing the fleet beforehand.

- Airing your differences with another cruiser at a social function or on the VHF.
- Discussing sensitive subject material on the morning cruiser net.
- Borrowing money, and being asked to pay it back.
- Any anti-social behavior as it pertains to the harmony of the fleet.

This all may sound a bit extreme, although we would hope not. Most of the codes of etiquette should be common sense. Harmonious behavior is a required condition for successful cruising. There is a quick-acting karma found while cruising. If a cruiser is rude, mean spirited, or antagonistic to the occupants of a harbor, there will be no safety net to catch them when the inevitable fall comes.

One cruiser had such a bad reputation for his dishonesty and guard-dog mentality, word of his arrivals and departures spread faster than a strong north wind. Another couple was so cutting and abrasive toward others, people began to avoid them and those functions they attended. It was not long before they pulled up their anchor and made a quick exit from the harbor. People do not go through such lengths necessary for cruising, to end up tolerating obnoxious behavior which pollutes their paradise.

Even the aspect of borrowing from a fellow cruiser takes on a new dimension, one we do not deal with in the States. Since most items in foreign ports are not easy to come by, the person who lent you the item must go to great lengths to find a replacement, whether it be locating a ride to the nearest town, or the funds required to replace what was borrowed. Be aware of the circumstances and always assume that anything borrowed should be replaced. If you are in doubt, don't hesitate to ask.

The old adage—what goes around comes around— is a cruiser's golden rule. Replacing or reimbursing for loaned gear is proper etiquette, especially considering the diversity of budgets in the fleet. Some folks would think nothing of spending $70 in a given day, while other cruisers cannot afford to spend $70 in a week. Believe it or not, many cruisers have budgeted even less and we were one of them.

Don't think for a moment that budget cruisers cannot participate in social gatherings. Many of them

Thou Shalt Not ...

Some codes found in the cruising community are age-old and have been written in stone long ago. In the modern era, some of these social rules appear to have become lax. Not so in the cruising community. It is a bit old-fashioned when it comes to respect for the family circle.

Do not covet your neighbor's spouse, girlfriend, boyfriend or 18-year-old son or daughter. Hopefully that covers all the bases. We were

somewhat surprised at this "code of conduct" we observed, early on in the game.

It took us a while to formulate an opinion on what was very obvious, while attending social gatherings.

Flirting amongst couples, even with drink and merriment, was not excessive or even acceptable as we now conclude. What was curious was the fact that these folks were by no means puritans.

Relationships in this lifestyle are held in high re-may pass up a night of dining in town, but almost everyone looks forward to the potluck dinner. Potluck dinners and sunset coffee exchanges provide a way for all members of the fleet to get to know each other.

Potluck dinners in the cruising environment can become giant feasts for both the pallet and the mind. We have witnessed some incredible gourmet dishes at these events. Both the food and attendants are varied like no other. Even potlucks, however, contain an element of etiquette.

The general rule of thumb is to prepare enough contribution to feed twice the number of your crew. Some of the great favorites at potluck events are fresh baked breads and sweets, and any familiar items from home which are difficult to find in foreign environments. Whether it's the classic Twinkie or some fresh Parmesan cheese, these items will be the first to

gard and value. Folks who have learned to live together in close quarters and who have experienced some of the not so fun parts of this game, have become almost single entities as much as they have grown as individuals.

The moral of this message is, if you're predisposed to flirting, be aware it could stop your cruising experience dead in its tracks. Cruisers tend to be open and willing to communicate across the gender lines. Those new to the cruising community should not mistake this openness for anything more than platonic friendship. A quick way of excluding yourself from the community is to conduct yourself with the attitude that anyone who is uncommonly friendly with you puts them on a "hit list".

There is one more taboo, of equal consequence: Not rendering assistance to another vessel in distress. We can think of no quicker way, other than the aforementioned taboo, to be ostracized from (Continued on Page 182) go. One potluck was fondly recalled for months after homemade ice cream was served. Certainly one need not go to such lengths, most cruisers are thrilled simply to consume something that deviates from their usual diet. Anything that provides a new experience is often a hit as well. We had the opportunity to try moray eel and octopus soup at one potluck. Neither of us really cared for those items, but to say we tried it sounds daring.

Fare that will not make you stand out from the crowd include rice, beans, nachos, or a heaping plate full of sprouts. Most of us consume these items on a daily basis down south, and simply have lost our initial excitement over them. It is our sincere hope that new folks, at least during potlucks, do stand

---

(Continued from Page 181)
the community.

If there is any one action to illustrate the character of a group or individual, it is the willingness to get involved for the sake of helping another vessel in distress. Conversely, there is probably no better way to outcast oneself from the cruising community and lifestyle, than to be marked as a person who does not get involved in the emergency of a fellow cruiser. We have personally witnessed another cruiser sit by and watch others rescue a dragging vessel, one that was bearing down on his own, and do nothing, not even offer a word of thanks to those who averted disaster. This lack of action was not only noted by others, it was also passed on as necessary information to the rest of the fleet.

There are other taboos which can adversely effect one's experience in the lifestyle. The two we chose to mention at length were ones that we observed and found to be a common topic of discussion among friends.

apart from the crowd. We are all getting a little tired of the "new and improved" bean and rice soufflés.

If asked to another cruiser's vessel for dinner or evening coffee, be prepared to bring a little something along for the hosts. If you drink alcohol, the B.Y.O.B. rule usually applies. And although it is not a rule of the road, it is considerate to bring your own plates and utensils. Water conservation is the main reason, not so much an unwillingness to wash dirty dishes.

Water, even when readily available, still requires a dinghy ride to its source and the effort needed to haul it back on board. Speaking from experience, we have always been impressed when someone has been considerate enough to alleviate some of our efforts.

Does this mean we would adversely judge a guest who used our dishes? Of course not. It is just one of the details that make certain guests stand out as ultra-thoughtful folks. It is also advisable to remember that it is in good taste to reciprocate with a like invitation for dinner. You will find that the most considerate folks you meet are also the ones with lots of dinners to attend. ⚓

The true pearls of Mexico are the people. Kindness and generosity, along with countless smiles welcomed us at each stop.

Chapter 12
On the Road to Paradise

The World You Take is the World You'll Make

To see a World in a grain of sand, And a heaven in a wild flower,
Hold infinity in the palm of your hand, And eternity in an hour.
—William Blake

Despite some exaggerated rumors, knowledgeable travelers have been safely experiencing the beautiful Baja peninsula for years. Prior to us running off to explore this spectacular wonderland we too suffered through countless warnings of peril at the hands of thugs and corrupt officials. Friends and family cautioned us against proceeding with our plans.

Fortunately, this advice was tossed to the wind, and over the course of our voyage we discovered the true pearl of Mexico. Although the heart-stopping sunsets and pure, empty beaches enticed us into staying, it was the people of the Baja that made us fall in love with the country. Needless to say, no bandits were encountered. Kindness and generosity, along with countless smiles welcomed us at each stop.

Checking in and out at the major ports, a procedure where boaters present their documents to the local port captain, allowed us ample contact with officials in the Baja. During our cruise we also encountered representatives of the navy, local police and other federal employees. The majority of them proved to be both courteous and considerate, and were quick to offer assistance.

While based in Puerto Escondido, we experienced our first and only boarding by the Mexican Navy. Although the sight of armed soldiers coming aboard was unnerving at first, the experience proved positive. They simply checked our paperwork and took a look down below. They were friendly and quick about their business. A friend's vessel reported later that when they were boarded, the soldiers would not go below decks in fear of scuffing the shiny, wooden floors.

Even though that was the only official encounter we had with the navy, their presence was a constant since a naval outpost is located at the entrance of Puerto Escondido. In fact, during baseball games held on Sunday, we came to count on the few naval officers who showed up to volunteer their powerful swings at bat.

The police and port officials of Loreto have also been just as friendly and helpful. Numerous boat rescues were coordinated and acted out by port captain personnel, locals, and cruisers sailing in the vicinity.

Although we rarely heard of any thievery and personally never experienced any, one unlucky couple visiting the Baja did lose an unlocked bicycle. When they reported the loss to the police department, they were impressed by the efficiency of the local officials. Although their bike was never recovered, many items are found and returned to their respective owners.

Spending time in the Baja makes it very easy to drop your stateside paranoia. Much of the local charm is earned by their trusting nature. Small tiendas throughout the peninsula often use old cigar boxes as cash registers. The overflowing box of pesos is stored on a counter right behind the check-out stand within view. Indeed, honesty appears to be one of the residents' greatest attributes, along with their generosity and willingness to help.

Of all the sea stories retold by the gringos touring this grand peninsula, the most common is about fishermen dropping part of their bounty off to foreign visitors. Although we certainly appreciated the gift of a huge red snapper from a fisherman, we were completely amazed when we were presented with a lobster by another.

Just as willing as the locals share their food with visitors, they will also come to your aid when trouble arises. During our voyage down the Pacific side of the peninsula, we became dangerously low on fuel. A passing shrimping trawler offered to give us enough fuel to safely reach the port.

Throughout our time in the Baja, we also covered many miles in our beat-up convertible. On this mostly barren highway, it was comforting to see the Green Angel rescue vehicles frequently during each of our trips. They exist to aid stranded motorists, along with their out of commission vehicles.

We were fortunate enough to avoid any breakdowns, but one friend we met was not as lucky. The good news is, when his vehicle left him stranded, a local came to his aid, while American tourists just passed him by. Not only did his rescuer locate a needed part requiring a drive miles out of his way, he also helped with the installation.

Stories of local assistance like this are commonplace, leading many seasoned travelers to conclude that the locals are surely the best resource the Baja has to offer. They have been the true jewels of our adventures. Add the fine ingredients of magical landscapes and fiery sunsets, and we can think of no other place we would rather be.

However, if a visitor carries a bad attitude across the border, while forgetting his manners, a different experience is more likely. Of the many adjustments a new cruiser needs to make, awareness of the customs and culture of the host country visited is one of the most important.

Some of the nicest cruisers we have met still seemed unable to adapt to, or at least accept the customs of the people in whose country they found their paradise. Both criticism and complaints toward services or the lack thereof have been heard. Rude and ignorant comments are sometimes made during times of adversity. It is of utmost importance to realize that when you travel to different lands you are governed by different rules. If you want to fully enjoy your travel experiences and avoid any unnecessary difficulties, you have the power within. Simply respect your hosts and act accordingly.

Life does move slowly south of the border, which is one of the major attractions to most visitors. We have grown to appreciate their differences, adopting some as our own.

In a land where it is difficult to gain wealth financially, its residents have looked toward the natural resources for wealth, those of family and community. From what we have seen, they are moved by kindness, mutual respect and a playfulness seen in children and adults alike. A willingness to be open, and a sincere interest to get to know the people adds dimension and quality to an already life altering journey. They certainly added much to ours.

Appreciating the people you will encounter on your cruise is the easy part of Cruising 101, and one of the most pleasurable. The other lessons involved in the cruising lifestyle may come harder.

After those first trying months, most of your time will be spent figuring out how to get the salt on your margarita and how to avoid doing the wash one more week. And each and every day you will look up to the heavens and thank God you never gave up.

There is still much for us to learn from our experiences, even after Cruising 101. We have not yet perfected all of the nautical knots, but one we finally did manage to tie was our own. With a giant potluck and Captain Blackie from the vessel *Love* to do the rites, we exchanged vows overlooking our little hidden harbor. The journey always continues.

We sure hope you pass your class with honors. Remember, there is always the graduate school of cruising and one day we will be there, continuing our lessons. For the time being, however, we will apply our knowledge, and always remember to be kind to each other and hope you do the same. Fair winds and safe harbors. ⚓

Order Form

Need Another Copy?

Please send a check or money order for $17.95, plus tax if applicable. Include $2 for shipping. Make check payable to Free Fall Press.

Free Fall Press
Post Office Box 7887
San Diego, CA 92167

Name: _____

Address: _____

City: _____

Telephone: _____

Sales tax:
Please add 7.75% for books shipped to California addresses.

Shipping:
$2.00 for the first book and $1.00 for each additional book.

Payment:
Checks and Money orders accepted.